access to history

BRITAIN: DOMESTIC POLITICS 1918–39

Second Edition

Robert Pearce

Hodder & Stoughton

A MEMBER OF THE HODDER HEADLINE GROUP

Acknowledgements

The front cover shows Stanley Baldwin by R.G. Eves, reproduced courtesy of the National Portrait Gallery, London.

The publishers would like to thank the following individuals, institutions and companies for permission to reproduce copyright illustrations in this book:
Illustrated London News, pages 12, 43, 50; 'The Builders', Punch, page 123; 'The Hatching' originally published in *The Star*, David Low, 1921, © Solo Syndication & Literary Agency, Centre for the Study of Cartoons and Caricature, University of Kent at Canterbury page 23; David Low, *Evening Standard*, 30/11/1929, © Solo Syndication & Literary Agency, Centre for the Study of Cartoons and Caricature, University of Kent at Canterbury page 75.

The publishers would also like to thank the following for permission to reproduce material in this book:
Sunday Dispatch in Fleet Sheet, Press Barons and Politics: The Journals of Collin Brooks, 1932–1940, ed. N.J. Crowson, Camden, Fifth Series, Vol. 11, Royal Historical Society, 1998.

Every effort has been made to trace and acknowledge ownership of copyright. The publishers will be glad to make suitable arrangements with any copyright holders whom it has not been possible to contact.

Orders: please contact Bookpoint Ltd, 78 Milton Park, Abingdon, Oxon OX14 4TD. Telephone (44) 01235 827720, Fax: (44) 01235 400454. Lines are open from 9.00–6.00, Monday to Saturday, with a 24 hour message answering service. Email address: orders@bookpoint.co.uk

British Library Cataloguing in Publication Data
A catalogue record for this title is available from the British Library

ISBN 0 340 78256 0

First published 1992
Impression number   10 9 8 7 6 5 4 3 2
Year   2005 2004 2003 2002 2001

Typeset by Fakenham Photosetting Limited, Fakenham, Norfolk
Printed in Great Britain for Hodder & Stoughton Educational, a division of Hodder Headline Plc, 338 Euston Road, London NW1 3BH by Redwood Books Ltd.

Contents

Preface

To the general reader

Although the *Access to History* series has been designed with the needs of students studying the subject at higher examination levels very much in mind, it also has a great deal to offer the general reader. The main body of the text (i.e. ignoring the 'Study Guides' at the ends of chapters) forms a readable and yet stimulating survey of a coherent topic as studied by historians. However, each author's aim has not merely been to provide a clear explanation of what happened in the past (to interest and inform): it has also been assumed that most readers wish to be stimulated into thinking further about the topic and to form opinions of their own about the significance of the events that are described and discussed (to be challenged). Thus, although no prior knowledge of the topic is expected on the reader's part, she or he is treated as an intelligent and thinking person throughout. The author tends to share ideas and possibilities with the reader, rather than passing on numbers of so-called 'historical truths'.

To the student reader

Although advantage has been taken of the publication of a second edition to ensure the results of recent research are reflected in the text, the main alteration from the first edition is the inclusion of new features, and the modification of existing ones, aimed at assisting you in your study of the topic at AS level, A level and Higher. Two features are designed to assist you during your first reading of a chapter. The *Points to Consider* section following each chapter title is intended to focus your attention on the main theme(s) of the chapter, and the issues box following most section headings alerts you to the question or questions to be dealt with in the section. The *Working on . . .* section at the end of each chapter suggests ways of gaining maximum benefit from the chapter.

There are many ways in which the series can be used by students studying History at a higher level. It will, therefore, be worthwhile thinking about your own study strategy before you start your work on this book. Obviously, your strategy will vary depending on the aim you have in mind, and the time for study that is available to you.

If, for example, you want to acquire a general overview of the topic in the shortest possible time, the following approach will probably be the most effective:

1. Read chapter 1. As you do so, keep in mind the issues raised in the *Points to Consider* section.

2. Read the *Points to Consider* section at the beginning of chapter 2 and decide whether it is necessary for you to read this chapter.
3. If it is, read the chapter, stopping at each heading or sub-heading to note down the main points that have been made. Often, the best way of doing this is to answer the question(s) posed in the *Key Issues* boxes.
4. Repeat stage 2 (and stage 3 where appropriate) for all the other chapters.

If, however, your aim is to gain a thorough grasp of the topic, taking however much time is necessary to do so, you may benefit from carrying out the same procedure with each chapter, as follows:

1. Try to read the Chapter in one sitting. As you do this, bear in mind any advice given in the *Points to Consider* section.
2. Study the flow diagram at the end of the chapter, ensuring that you understand the general 'shape' of what you have just read.
3. Read the *Working on …* section and decide what further work you need to do on the chapter. In particularly important sections of the book, this is likely to involve reading the chapter a second time and stopping at each heading and sub-heading to think about (and probably to write a summary of) what you have just read.
4. Attempt the *Source-based questions* section. It will sometimes be sufficient to think through your answers, but additional understanding will often be gained by forcing yourself to write them down.

When you have finished the main chapters of the book, study the 'Further Reading' section and decide what additional reading (if any) you will do on the topic.

This book has been designed to help make your studies both enjoyable and successful. If you can think of ways in which this could have been done more effectively, please contact us. In the meantime, we hope that you will gain greatly from your study of History.

Keith Randell & Robert Pearce

1

Introduction: The Shape of British Politics, 1918–39

POINTS TO CONSIDER

This chapter provides a brief introduction to the key themes and individuals of the interwar period. Try to grasp the main issues and controversies – and avoid making up your mind about them until you have read the succeeding chapters.

KEY DATES

1918 The Representation of the People Act: votes for men at 21 and women at 30.
1926 The general strike.
1928 Women received the vote on the same terms as men.
1929 Onset of economic depression.
1939 Start of the Second World War.

1 The Political Scene

KEY ISSUE What were the new features of British politics after the First World War?

The year 1918 marks a vital turning point in British political history. From this time onwards we can properly talk of 'democracy' in Britain – rule of the people by the people, or at least by a large majority of them. The Representation of the People Act of February 1918 gave the vote to women over the age of 30 and to those men over 21 who had not already been enfranchised. In the elections of 1910 about 7.5 million men had been able to vote, roughly 60 per cent of 'adult' (over 21) males – or less than 30 per cent of all adults in Britain. In 1918, in sharp contrast, there were over 21 million electors, including 8 million women – about 78 per cent of the adult population. The new reform act also specified that women could stand as parliamentary candidates; that there was to be a maximum of five years, as opposed to the previous seven, between elections; and that these contests were to be held on a single day, instead of being spread out over a week or two as previously. It also laid down that a candidate would have to pay a deposit of £150, to be forfeit if he or she failed to attract one-eighth of the total votes cast. Various forms of proportional representation were also considered in 1918, but they were rejected as too complicated. Modern British democracy would therefore employ the 'first past the post' system.

Further reforms were to follow. In 1928 women received the vote on precisely the same terms as men, so that everybody aged 21 and over could vote except peers, lunatics and felons. In 1948 'plural voting' came to an end: no longer could graduates cast a second vote for one of the 12 university seats in Britain, and neither could owners of business premises outside their constituency of residence vote twice. Finally, in 1969 the voting age was lowered to 18. But the 1918 legislation, in conjunction with earlier reforms (for example, the payment of MPs and the limiting of the powers of the House of Lords to delaying bills for a maximum of two years, both in 1911), was important enough to mark the real breakthrough into the era of modern mass democracy. We are today the heirs of the reforms of 1918.

Back in the nineteenth century the electorate was small, MPs were unpaid amateurs and each constituency was largely self-contained, fighting an election without much regard for the national parties – or, indeed, not fighting at all. In the general election of 1900, when the prime minister and the foreign secretary were both members of the House of Lords, 35 per cent of MPs were returned unopposed. In 1918 this old system was swept away, and in 1929 only seven MPs were elected unopposed. Power shifted irrevocably to the Commons.

1918 was a political turning point in other ways too. In this year the First World War ended. During the war the government had been forced to interfere in the lives of British citizens and intervene in the economy much more than ever before, and never again would governments be able to relapse into traditional, nineteenth-century *laissez-faire*, though some would have liked to do so. Governments were responsible to the people and – to some degree – had to give the people what they wanted. Governments still had their traditional imperial and foreign policy concerns, but now they would be judged much more on their economic policies. Governments would take the credit or blame – whether deserved or not – for rises or falls in living standards.

The war had other effects as well. Economically, it accelerated Britain's decline. Britain had been the first country to undergo the 'industrial revolution' and had thereby achieved an economic predominance in the world out of all proportion to its size and natural resources. Some decline was inevitable, as larger rivals with richer raw materials (especially Germany and the USA) appeared on the scene and borrowed and perfected Britain's industrial techniques. But the war now accelerated this process of relative economic downturn (*relative* because in absolute terms British output still expanded and the standard of living improved).

Politicians in the twentieth century had to operate against this economic background. Successful statesmanship had to involve several factors: accepting the reality of Britain's relative decline (never an easy psychological task); minimising or slowing down the decline (an even more difficult operation); and, if possible, disguising the unpleasant reality as something more palatable (work of the utmost complexity). Retreats had to be presented, whenever possible, as advances. A supreme example of this was to be the rationalisation of the loss of the Empire as the founding of the Commonwealth.

Politically, the war hastened the decline of the Liberal party and boosted the position of Labour. There were no Liberal governments after the war, while Labour formed two governments (both minority administrations) in 1924 and 1929–31. Otherwise the Conservatives formed governments themselves or controlled coalitions. The interwar period was therefore heavily dominated by the Conservative party.

2 Interwar Politicians

> **KEY ISSUE** How able and constructive were the leading politicians?

Until quite recently the overwhelming consensus among historians has been that politicians after 1918 did their work badly and were failures. To some extent this is due to the country's poor economic performance. In Britain the so-called 'Roaring Twenties' failed to roar: there was high unemployment throughout the decade, a general strike in 1926, and in 1929 the onset of the most severe depression of modern times. Yet the 1930s, the 'Hungry Thirties', are said to have been even worse, characterised by longer dole queues, by the 'depressed areas' and the 'hunger marches' to London. Nor was the problem simply economic. Many young intellectuals turned from what they saw as the moral bankruptcy and decadence of Britain to the brave new world of communism and Soviet Russia. The picture could scarcely be more depressing – but it was to become so. For in the late 1930s British politicians appeased Nazi Germany and led Britain into a war which (so the indictment continues) could have been avoided if they had stood up to Hitler instead of pandering to him.

a) The Case against the Politicians

The case for the prosecution against the interwar politicians runs as follows. After the war, the political system in Britain showed great stability – but this was not a virtue. Politics became a sort of game, as shown by the highly elaborate ritual of parliamentary procedure: political power had become an end in itself, dangerously divorced from the real problems and needs of Britain. Lloyd George won the general election at the end of the war by cynically promising the electorate what he knew he could not deliver. Here was a talented man whose abilities were far higher than those of his contemporaries, but a man devoid of principle. He split the Liberal party and almost split the Conservatives; he was corrupt and lowered the standards of British political life (see chapter 2). In 1922 he was jettisoned by the Conservatives, but there was no real improvement, only a different kind of failure. He was succeeded by arch-mediocrities: Andrew Bonar Law, Stanley Baldwin and Neville Chamberlain in the Conservative party and Ramsay MacDonald from Labour ranks (see chapters 3–5). Charles Loch Mowat has said that after Lloyd George came 'rule by pygmies', men without vision or truly constructive abilities, men who fiddled while Britain declined and Europe caught fire.

No one remembers Bonar Law, the 'unknown prime minister'. Baldwin is said to have been lazy, with a talent only for wishful thinking. He achieved high office by luck and kept it by good fortune. MacDonald had a fine presence – and a first-rate ability for saying nothing with great eloquence. Chamberlain was another unimaginative mediocrity, blessed with an entirely unfounded certainty that he always knew best. The only talent of these men seemed to be a capacity to fool the electorate into voting for them – but then the choice for the voters was limited. The electorate was presented with an effective choice (or should it be an ineffective one?) between the Conservative and Labour parties, both of which in practice followed a consensus that avoided radical policies or significant changes. Labour talked of socialism as an entirely new system of society, but in reality this was reserved not for this year or even next year but for sometime and perhaps never. In 1931, during the greatest and most controversial political crisis of the interwar period, the disguise was removed and MacDonald set up an all-party National Government, which continued to provide more of the same unwholesome political diet. Some said MacDonald had planned such a government all along (see chapter 4).

The charges are quite devastating. And it must be admitted that it can be emotionally satisfying to denigrate famous figures from the past. The dead do make easy targets! Yet the primary concern of the historian should surely be to understand rather than to judge. While it is legitimate to be critical of interwar politicians, it should be recognised that there are more favourable ways of assessing the politics of 1918–39.

b) The Case for the Politicians

The case for the defence begins by pointing out that the charges made against interwar politicians are extravagant. They imply that politicians had greater powers than they really did. Britain's relative economic decline had profound causes rooted in the past, and politicians could do little to change the long established pattern. It followed from this that Britain did not have the wealth or the power to dominate European diplomacy. Appeasement was therefore a sensible policy: politicians, quite naturally, attempted to avoid a war in which this country had everything to lose and nothing to gain. The critics thus concentrate too much on the role of individuals and ignore the real problems governments had to face.

Journalists are in the business of making snap, black-and-white judgements: historians aspire to a deeper understanding based on more complete evidence. When C.L. Mowat (1955) and A.J.P. Taylor (1965) wrote their profoundly influential, and indeed brilliant, surveys of interwar politics the official government papers were closed to scholars. They wrote while the 50-year rule was still in operation: government papers were released only after an interval of 50 years. Hence they were unable to see governments 'from the inside' and sympathetically. The 30-year rule, adopted in 1967, has allowed historians to look afresh at the period 1918–39 and to appreciate much more fully the perceptions of ministers themselves, the problems they faced and the constraints that limited their actions.

Much fuller studies of the interwar politicians have now been made: and the leading figures emerge as multi-dimensional characters, no longer dwarfed by the 'great' figures of the Victorian and Edwardian eras. Nor does the interwar period, from a present-day perspective, seem such a time of failure. The maintenance of parliamentary democracy was itself a considerable achievement. In no general election after 1918 did less than 70 per cent of the electorate turn out to vote. The public retained its confidence in democracy. In contrast, on the continent of Europe, democracy collapsed in Italy, Germany, Austria and elsewhere. Many Europeans must have admired the resilience and stability of British political institutions at a time of unparalleled upheaval elsewhere.

3 Conclusion

> **KEY ISSUE** How is the period between the wars best interpreted?

It is possible to view the period 1918–39 in sharply contrasting ways, and to be 'for' or 'against' the politicians of the interwar years. It is also possible – and perhaps more desirable – to seek to give a balanced account. But this is not easy, for many myths survive about these years. One is the idea of the 'Hungry Thirties', which is actually no more than a very partial truth. In an unguarded moment George Orwell wrote of 'pre-1939 normality (with 3 million unemployed, etc)'. But 3 million was the *worst*, not the normal or average, total of unemployed in Britain between the wars. All too often the worst has been depicted as interwar normality. The 1920s and 1930s did see the hunger marches and the depressed areas, and no one should ignore them or the human tragedy they represented. But these decades saw boom as well as bust, and especially a growth in new consumer goods industries. Many people's lives were substantially improved between the wars. There were in a sense several Englands, and each must be given due consideration. The difficulty is that it is all too easy to mistake the part for the whole. One of the hardest tasks of the historian is to decide what is representative of an age and what is exceptional.

All too often the interwar years have been caricatured. One aspect has been magnified out of proper proportion, so that other aspects have been unjustly minimised or ignored altogether. For instance, the political consensus that produced the national government and led to its overwhelming victory in the 1931 election has too often monopolised attention, leading historians to overlook the political ferment which energised left and right in the 1930s and produced the British Union of Fascists and the Socialist League (see chapter 6). The interwar years were not a completely sterile, wasted period. They were years of acute political controversy in which Britain became a mass democracy. There was stability in some senses, and especially in terms of political personnel. But the Liberal party, which had helped govern Britain in the nineteenth century and from 1906 to 1922, went into decline; and the Labour party, which had won only 40 seats in 1910, achieved sufficient electoral support to form two minority governments between the wars. The Conservatives seemed to go on forever; but a long period of domination by Stanley Baldwin – a man with more virtues than his critics have recognised, and more faults than his admirers have admitted – saw intense strife within the Conservative party.

1918–39 is of great importance in the development of modern British politics – and indeed of modern Britain, for we cannot study 'pure' political history. Politics is not a self-contained political game (speeches and votes, party intrigues, offices and honours, the egotism of those who climb to the top of the 'greasy pole'); indeed, the more it is like this, the more a political system becomes decadent. Politics should not be an end in itself, but a means to an end – a means to 'good government'. True democracy is government 'for', as well as 'of' and 'by', the people. The business of politics should be to obtain and retain power in order to grapple with the problems that beset a country, and therefore politicians need to be men of vision and humanity as well as competent legislators and administrators. It follows that 'political history' must involve social and economic history, diplomacy and international relations. (Geoffrey Elton once called political history 'a portmanteau affair, a vacuum cleaner sucking in the products of other forms of historical study.') Other books in this series focus on foreign and imperial affairs, on industrial relations

and socio-economic issues. It is from them that a 'rounded' understanding of these topics will be acquired. But such issues are inevitably
an integral part of political history, and they have been included –
sometimes only in brief – in this volume. It is this diversity that makes
politics such an interesting and intensely difficult and challenging
study.

Disraeli once said that 'the vicissitudes of politics are inexhaustible'; and the twists and turns of political history are also a
source of inexhaustible fascination. There are no easy or final
answers about the politics or politicians of the interwar period, for
debate and disagreement are at the heart of the study of history.
History has been called 'an unending dialogue' between the past
and the present, and as such it provides us with unlimited scope for
our talents as historians.

Summary Diagram
The Shape of British Politics, 1918–39

Constitution	Governments	Economy
1911 Payment of MPs		
1911 Parliament Act, limiting powers of the House of Lords		First World War – end of *laissez faire*
1918 Representation of the People Act a. Votes for all men over 21 and all women over 30; b. elections to be held on on day; c. 'First past post' system – no proportional representation	1918–22 The Lloyd George Coalition – Conservatives and some Liberals 1922–4 Conservative Govt. under Bonar Lar (1922–3) and Baldwin (1923–4)	1920s – 1 million unemployed – 10% of insured work-force
	1924 Labour Govt. (minority) under MacDonald	
1928 Representation of the People Act Votes for all men and women over 21 except peers, lunatics and felons	1924–9 Conservative Govt. under Baldwin	1926 – General Strike
	1929–31 Labour Govt. (minority) under MacDonald	1929 – onset of Great Depression
	1931–5 National Govt. – Coalition mainly Conservative under MacDonald (1931–5) and Baldwin (1935 onwards)	1930s – mass unemployment (3 million in 1932); growth of consumer goods industries
	1935–9 National Govt. under Baldwin (1935–7) and Chamberlain (1937–9)	

Working on Chapter I

Your notes on this chapter should be very brief and mainly made up of headings. You will be able to fill in the details as you read later chapters. Try to do two things: a) map out the 'shape' of the period you are about to study, and b) outline the main controversies of the interwar period. In particular you should summarise the two main 'schools of thought' – that which is highly critical of interwar politicians and that which tends to praise or defend them. A grasp of the main ideas is far more essential, at this stage, than specific details.

As you read the succeeding chapters, you should try to see each government within the broad context of the interwar years as a whole and keep coming back to the central issue of how well or how badly politicians grappled with Britain's problems.

2 The Lloyd George Coalition, 1916–22

POINTS TO CONSIDER

This chapter deals with the very crowded years when Lloyd George was prime minister. You need to acquire a knowledge of the events of these years, but try to keep in mind two issues: the degree of success or failure of the government's policies, and why Lloyd George fell from power in 1922.

KEY DATES

1914 (August) start of the First World War: Asquith's Liberal government in office.

1915 (May) coalition formed, LG as Minister of Munitions.

1916 (April) Easter Rising in Dublin; (July–Nov.) Battle of the Somme; (Dec.) Asquith resigned, LG as PM.

1917 Germans began unrestricted submarine warfare; (April) USA entered the war.

1918 (Feb.) Representation of the People Act; (11 Nov.) end of the war; (14 Dec.) coalition victory in the general election.

1919 (January) strike in Glasgow: troops sent in; (28 June) signing of the Treaty of Versailles.

1920 Agriculture Act, guaranteeing minimum prices; Unemployment Insurance Act, covering almost 12 million people; (March) failure of LG's attempt at 'fusion'; (21 Nov.) 'Bloody Sunday':15 Britons and 12 Irish killed.

1921 (April) threatened general strike by Triple Alliance; (May) resignation of Bonar Law, Austen Chamberlain as new Conservative leader; (July) resignation of Addison from coalition; (July) truce in Ireland after Anglo-Irish war; (6 Dec.) Anglo-Irish Treaty signed.

1922 (Feb.) Geddes Axe, cuts of £64 million; (April) Genoa conference, a failure; (June) assassination of Ulster MP Sir Henry Wilson; (July) Honours Scandal; (19 Oct.) Carlton Club meeting, resignation of Lloyd George, Bonar Law as PM.

1 Background: Lloyd George and the War-time Coalition

> **KEY ISSUE** What impact did the Lloyd George coalition have on Britain's war effort?

The First World War began in August 1914. Its political consequences for Britain were to be profound: it was eventually to test the Liberal government of the day beyond its capacity for survival. Yet at first it was hoped that the war would be essentially a naval affair, in which the might of the royal navy would be decisive. Certainly it was believed that it would be all over by Christmas. The Prime Minister, Herbert Asquith, assumed that the admirals and generals would produce a rapid victory. But in reality the only possible knock-out blow was a German one, as the enemy attempted to operate the Schlieffen plan – to defeat the French swiftly and then move eastwards to meet the larger but more slowly mobilising Russian force, and so avoid fighting a war on two fronts. The battle of the Marne in September 1914 halted the German army and destroyed this strategy. The war of *movement* was now over. Troops dug themselves in on the western front. It was stalemate. The front line established in November 1914 did not change by more than ten miles in any direction until 1917. A tremendously destructive and expensive war of attrition had begun.

Asquith had been a formidable political figure in his earlier days. Certainly no one had contested his right to succeed to the premiership when ill-health had forced Campbell-Bannerman to resign in April 1908. But by 1914 he had lost his grip. Some said he drank too much. No one ever claimed that he was actually drunk, but one observer said he was sometimes 'exhilarated' and another that he was 'sodden'. His aloofness and detachment infuriated some of his colleagues, and he seemed unable to adapt to the new conditions. He appointed Lord Kitchener, the hero of the 1898 battle of Omdurman, Secretary of State for War. This was a poor choice, for Kitchener excelled only as a recruiting poster. Otherwise there were no changes of political personnel. It was, in the Prime Minister's complacent words, 'business as usual.'

Yet by the beginning of 1915 it was clear that the war would last a long time and that the 'home front' would be as important for the war effort as the front line. In particular there would have to be sustained attempts to recruit more men and produce more weapons. Change at the top was needed; and shell shortages, together with the failure of the Gallipoli campaign in the Dardanelles (a brave but misconceived attempt to find an eastern solution to the stalemate on the western front), lowered the government's prestige so that in May 1915 a coalition was virtually forced on Asquith. He was faced with a choice between resignation and acceptance of an all-party coalition. He chose the latter.

Key changes were now made. Lloyd George (widely known as 'LG') became Minister of Munitions. He had long been the most dynamic Liberal minister and seemed to show that the Liberal party was not doomed to decline, providing it could jettison its nineteenth century philosophy of *laissez-faire* and individualism. He believed the Liberal party had outgrown its original theories. And anyway for him actions spoke louder than principles. He went into immediate action, cutting through bureaucratic red tape and requisitioning a hotel for the new ministry. The Munitions of War Act gave him control of the armaments factories, as well as the power to outlaw strikes and lock-outs.

Leading Conservatives joined the new cabinet, as did Arthur Henderson from the Labour party. But the position was still not satisfactory. There were 23 cabinet ministers: even if these men had respected each other – which they did not – there were still too many for the prompt despatch of business. Nor was there harmony between the parties. All the most important offices were held by Liberals, and many Conservatives distrusted the Prime Minister. As a result, the war effort suffered. In particular, conscription was delayed. Compulsory national service was vitally important, not only to provide soldiers but

DAVID LLOYD GEORGE (1863–1945)

-Profile-

Brought up in rural north Wales, where his uncle was a shoemaker, Lloyd George became MP for Caernarvon Boroughs in 1890. He came to national prominence as an opponent of the Boer War and entered the cabinet as President of the Board of Trade in 1905. He was a reforming Chancellor of the Exchequer from 1908, once insisting: 'I want things done. I want dreams, but dreams which are realisable. I want aspirations and discontent leading to a real paradise and a real earth in which men can live here and now … Suffering is too close to me. Misery is too near and insistent. Injustice is too obvious and glaring.' He was responsible for introducing old age pensions in 1908 and national insurance in 1911, and it was he who took the lead in limiting the powers of the House of Lords, also in 1911. During the war he was successful as Minister of Munitions and then, from December 1916, as Prime Minister. A colleague summed him up at this time: he 'cares nothing for precedents and knows no principles, but he has fire in his belly, and that is what we want'. He believed war was too serious a business to be left to free market forces.

As Prime Minister from 1916 to 1922 he was a dynamic executive. He inspired devoted admirers, but many found him untrustworthy and some positively hated him. He fell in October 1922, never to return to office. To some, it was the end of an era, as power passed to smaller, duller men.

to ensure that skilled men stayed at home to produce weapons, but Asquith was slow to act. He and many old-fashioned Liberals wanted to win the war, but they would not accept the loss of personal freedom that winning would inevitably involve. They would not face the fact that the real choice lay between collective government action ('war socialism'), a negotiated settlement (which few would seriously consider) and defeat (too horrible for anyone to contemplate). Only in January 1916 was a limited measure of conscription accepted.

Meanwhile the slaughter on the western front continued. On 1 July 1916 British forces under General Haig attacked the German lines near the Somme. On the first day 21,000 British soldiers were killed. When the battle ended in November Britain had lost 418,000 troops, France 194,000 and Germany 650,000 – and all for a few miles of territory.

His critics judged that Asquith had not the stomach for war. Leading Conservatives said he must go. They wanted him replaced by the man who had once seemed their greatest enemy, the radical Lloyd George. As Minister of Munitions, Lloyd George was the one undoubted success of the coalition, and when Kitchener died in June 1916 he took over as Secretary for War. It was put to Asquith that he should set up a three-man war cabinet with Lloyd George as chairman. Under these arrangements Asquith would still be called Prime Minister, but real power would lie with Lloyd George. Asquith would not accept this face-saving formula. Nor, since he was dependent on the support of Lloyd George and the leading Tories, could he simply ignore their advice and continue as before. In the end he chose to resign. He was too conscious of his dignity to serve under someone else: pride came before his fall.

Lloyd George became Prime Minister in December 1916. Patriotism, as much as ambition, had dictated his actions. But Asquith was now his enemy. In addition, most Liberal ministers resigned with their leader, and about half the Liberal MPs supported the old Prime Minister rather than the new. Never again was Lloyd George to belong to a major political party. He thus harmed his own political fortunes. Yet he benefited the country enormously. Lloyd George replacing Asquith, wrote one observer, was 'like substituting dynamite for a damp squib'.

A new sense of urgency produced immediate political changes. Lloyd George instituted a five-man war cabinet: himself, Conservative leader Andrew Bonar Law, Lords Curzon and Milner (two Conservatives with vast experience of effective administration in the empire), and Arthur Henderson from Labour ranks. It met almost every day. The able South African leader, Jan Smuts, sat in the war cabinet for a time, although he was not an MP. In fact there was a whole series of unorthodox appointments, as businessmen and experts generally were drafted into government. The historian H.A.L. Fisher, for instance, was brought in from Sheffield University as

President of the Board of Education, and Sir Joseph Maclay, a Glasgow shipowner, took over the Ministry of Shipping.

There were changes in administration too. An efficient cabinet secretariat was set up to co-ordinate government activities. Henceforth there was a proper cabinet agenda, as well as minutes of discussions and conclusions. Before this, cabinet meetings had been 'gentlemanly' (i.e. amateurish) affairs. In addition Lloyd George recruited a bevy of private secretaries from outside the ranks of the civil service. They occupied huts in the back garden of 10 Downing Street and were known, mockingly, as the 'garden suburb'. Some complained that the Prime Minister was acting unconstitutionally in by-passing the civil service and in extending the area of government control, as shipping, the railways and the mines were taken under state control. In addition, factories were told what they should be producing, prices were controlled, women took men's places in industry, food rationing was intensified, and a ministry of national service was set up to organise conscription effectively. It was said that Lloyd George was acting more like a president than a prime minister. He was not troubled by such views. Nor did he bother to act tactfully when he removed colleagues whom he considered not up to their tasks: he summarily sacked them. Of one failure he wrote, 'I don't care whether you drown him in a butt of Malmsey: he must be a dead chicken by tonight.' He was accumulating enemies, and thus storing up trouble for the future, but it was the needs of the present that were paramount. Constitutional niceties were ignored – what mattered was that government should be efficient and the war be won.

Lloyd George got things done, while his critics carped. His methods were strangely unorthodox, said some; inspired by no consistent political philosophy, said others. They were right. Yet the machine worked. Lloyd George's bold improvisations helped Britain to survive and ultimately to be on the winning side in the war.

One of the Prime Minister's main aims was to reverse the strategy of the generals – their determination to continue with the war of attrition despite the 'wastage' (their polite term for slaughter) that was its cost. In fact he achieved little, for the course of the war was already fixed. In July 1917 the third battle of Ypres ('Passchendaele') began. The Prime Minister believed it would be a disaster, and so it turned out, with 400,000 British casualties. He now acted to manoeuvre the commander of the imperial general staff, Sir William Robertson, into resigning. This created a full-scale political crisis. In the largely unwritten – and thus in a sense non-existent – British constitution, the power of a prime minister over the nation's generals was uncertain. Many Conservatives complained, as did Asquith and King George V. Only the complete support of Bonar Law enabled Lloyd George to ride the storm and survive. But he dared not treat General Haig in the same way. Lloyd George had a contempt for Haig, matched only by Haig's contempt for him. Years later he stopped in front of a portrait of Haig, immaculate in full dress uniform. 'He was brilliant,' he said, pointing to the top of a pair of military boots, 'up to there'. Instead, Lloyd George cleverly negated Haig's position by first forming a supreme war council (each allied prime minister and one colleague) to secure proper allied co-ordination, and secondly by establishing a unified Anglo-French command – a single supreme allied commander, the Frenchman, Marshal Foch.

Yet in fact Britain's war effort had of necessity to be largely a reaction to German initiatives. In February 1917 the German High Command announced a campaign of unrestricted submarine warfare: German submarines would attempt to sink all ships, including those of neutral nations, in the war zone around Britain and France. Britain faced catastrophe. In April 1917 attacks on American ships brought the USA into the war. The Germans expected this, but they believed that before the Americans could have any impact, Britain would be starved into submission and the war effectively ended.

Britain's food production was crucial. Lloyd George had already done much to improve matters. He established a minimum wage for farm labourers and also used prisoners of war to collect the harvest. The output of food increased significantly between 1916 and 1917. He also introduced food rationing – with one meatless day per week – and licensing hours, and insisted that beer should be watered down (in order to prevent 'the old habit of stupefaction by strong ales, which led to many being not perhaps drunk, but fuddled'). Yet German submarines threatened to destroy all this good work. In April 1917 allied and neutral shipping losses topped 850,000 tons: 430 ships were sunk and Britain was down to six weeks' supply of corn. In total, 3.3 million tons of shipping were lost between February and June 1917.

Lloyd George and his advisers decided that a convoy system should be introduced. Instead of crossing the Atlantic singly, merchant ships would go in groups, together with an armed escort. There was resistance at the Admiralty, but Lloyd George was adamant and had his way. Convoys soon proved a great success. Less than one per cent of escorted vessels were sunk, and by August the monthly shipping loss was down to 200,000 tons. The German strategy had failed, and the addition of the USA to the allied cause more than compensated for the loss of Russia, when the Bolsheviks pulled out of the conflict after their revolution in November 1917. The huge population and resources of the United States seemed to guarantee eventual victory against Germany.

There was one final German gamble – the Ludendorff offensive of the spring of 1918, during which German troops pushed to within 40 miles of Paris. When their advance was halted, the High Command faced the prospect of retreat followed by a war on German soil. Instead, on 11 November, a few days after Kaiser Wilhelm II had been persuaded to abdicate, an armistice was signed. A war which few had at first expected to last long had become one which many came to fear would go on forever. Now it came to an abrupt end.

2 The 'Coupon Election' and Politics after 1918

> **KEY ISSUE** Why, despite his great election victory in 1918, was Lloyd George's political position so vulnerable?

At the end of the First World War, few could be certain why the conflict had started or what Britain had been fighting for. No one was prepared to admit that it might have all been a meaningless accident. Instead, with great ingenuity, it was decided that the war was a 'war to end war' and that out of it would come a 'land fit for heroes'. In this way, something good would come out of the most destructive war in European history. 'We are at a turning point in our national history,' wrote one British commentator. 'We cannot return to the old ways, the old abuses, the old stupidities . . . We stand at the bar of history for judgement, and we shall be judged by the use we make of this unique opportunity.'

The politician who best embodied this new mood of confidence and determination was the Prime Minister, now widely praised as 'the man who won the war'. His pre-war activities also served him well, for no one had a better record in social reform. As Chancellor of the Exchequer LG had been responsible for a series of reforms which laid the basis for the welfare state in Britain. In 1908 he had introduced old age pensions, in 1909 a system of graduated income tax, and in 1911 his National Insurance Act had provided medical and unemployment insurance for the lowest paid workers in Britain.

Preparations for a general election were now quickly made. Lloyd George offered to make Asquith Lord Chancellor (with the power to choose two secretaries of state and six under-secretaries); but his former Liberal chief, and still leader of the official Liberal party, refused this generous offer. There was now no hope of re-uniting the Liberal party, and so Lloyd George was, in Beaverbrook's words, 'a prime minister without a party'. About 150 Liberal MPs were loyal to him, but he had to try to continue the coalition. The Labour party, whose representative Arthur Henderson had left the cabinet in 1917, would not participate, and even expelled the few Labour men who stayed on in the government. But the Conservatives were only too willing to accept. They had not won an election since 1902 and had, quite simply, lost confidence in themselves. They hoped to profit at the election from the Prime Minister's popularity. In December 1918 he had no trouble persuading them to continue a government which had been so successful since its formation in 1916. Indeed the Tory leader, Bonar Law, decided that Lloyd George could be 'prime minister for life, if he likes' – a predictions that turned out to be wildly inaccurate.

Neither the Tories nor Lloyd George paused long to consider whether the two groups were likely to be able to work together effectively in peacetime. During the war a common enemy, and thus a common national purpose, had united the parties. In the postwar period it would be immensely more difficult to achieve harmony. The cartoonist David Low represented the coalition by a strange, mule-like creature with a head at either end (see page 23): incapable of moving purposefully in any direction, it was reduced to going round in circles and thus getting nowhere. In other words, the coalition had no coherent political philosophy and was incapable of effective action. There is some truth in this judgement. But it ignores the successes the government was to achieve, and in December 1918 confidence was too great for much notice to be taken of the pessimists.

The new electoral registers were ready, and voting took place on Saturday 14 December. The result was announced two weeks later, after the soldiers' votes had been gathered. In fact only 2.7 million out of 3.9 million servicemen received ballot papers, and of these only one-third actually voted. Political apathy and cynicism affected many of those who had fought in the war, although as yet civilians were largely untouched. The turn-out was thus only 59 per cent of electors, the lowest in Britain this century; but because of the extension of the franchise to men over 21 and women over 30 (see page 1), the total vote cast was double that in the last election in 1910.

The 'coupon election' (so-called after the statement of support signed by Lloyd George and Bonar Law that coalition candidates received) has gone down in history as a disreputable and jingoistic affair. The Prime Minister did promise to 'make Germany pay' and to provide 'homes fit for heroes' but, overall, the campaign was more low-key and sober than is generally realised. *The Times* called the election 'the most orderly campaign of our time'.

Lloyd George dominated the hustings. A Liberal colleague wrote to him that there had never been an election like this 'in its one-man nature. Somebody said to me the other day that the only speeches in the papers were your speeches, that the only thing the country listened to was what you said.' Some historians claim that the election was essentially a plebiscite in favour of Lloyd George. In fact, had the election been a straightforward referendum for or against him, he would have lost, since more votes were cast against the coalition than for it. But the British electoral system – perhaps somewhat perversely – gave an overwhelming majority to the government.

The actual results were complicated, owing to splits within the parties and the uncertainty of some MPs' allegiances. Hence few books agree on exact totals.

The 'coupon' had proved remarkably effective, since 88 per cent of those endorsed – and thus unopposed by the other coalition groups

General Election, 14 December 1918			
Party	No. of votes	Percentage of total votes	Seats
Coalition Conservatives	3,504,198	32.6	335
Coalition Liberals	1,455,640	13.5	133
Coalition Labour	161,521	1.5	10
Coalition	**5,121,359**	**47.6**	**478**
Other Conservatives	370,375	3.4	23
Asquithian Liberals	1,298,808	12.1	28
Labour	2,385,472	2.2	63
Others	840,252	10.2	42
Sinn Fein	486,867	4.3	73

– were elected. This arrangement exaggerated the 'quirkiness' of the British electoral system, so that the number of seats won bore very little relationship to the votes cast. Labour, for instance, won almost a quarter of the votes but gained only 9 per cent of the seats, while the two wings of the Liberal party achieved similar popular votes but vastly different numbers of seats. The practical result of the election was a large majority for the coalition over all the other parties combined. In fact, since the Sinn Fein MPs refused to take their seats, the effective government majority was at least 322 – and won by a government with less than 50 per cent of the popular vote!

Asquith lost his seat, and so did three leading Labour figures, Arthur Henderson, James Ramsay MacDonald and Philip Snowden. The government was in an impregnable position, or so it seemed. But what of the enemy within? Could the two elements of the coalition – Conservatives and Lloyd George Liberals – co-operate effectively? In particular, Lloyd George was vulnerable. His was an inherently unstable position. He was a prime minister without a party, trapped in a political limbo or no man's land. How long could he command the support of the Conservative backbenchers? This was the key question. After all, the Tories by themselves would have a comfortable majority in parliament. He knew that their primary loyalty lay with their own party and that they would support him – a renegade Liberal – only so long as it was in their electoral interests to do so. He therefore had to maintain his popularity with the voting public. Only in this way could he convince the Conservatives that they depended on him, and not he on them. Hence he could not afford to delegate important tasks to his colleagues: instead he had always to be personally successful, and to be seen to be so. This was a dangerous strategy. Its corollary was that every political failure, as well as success, would be regarded as his own.

The cabinet reflected the predominance of the Conservatives. They now controlled nearly all the major offices and they therefore held sway. If Lloyd George was the driver – and one capable of high speed and some deft manoeuvres – he had nevertheless to follow a basic route mapped out by the Conservatives. Not that it often seemed like that to members of the majority party, who soon thought the Prime Minister too dominant. The Foreign Secretary, Lord Curzon, was to complain that Lloyd George used him as the 'gilded doormat'. The key figure in keeping the Conservative party loyal to the coalition was its leader, Andrew Bonar Law. He has been called the 'lynch-pin' of the coalition. Lloyd George and Bonar Law were contrasting figures – the one confident and enthusiastic, the other rather melancholy and pessimistic – but they liked each other and complemented each other. Baldwin judged that together they formed 'the most perfect partnership in political history'.

Bonar Law was a man of great ability and industry. It was said that as Chancellor of the Exchequer from 1916 to 1918 he did three or four men's work. Above all, he kept the Prime Minister informed of the opinions of the backbenchers. He was able to judge, almost unerringly, what they would accept and what they would not. Bonar Law's great skill was not so much leading the Conservatives as understanding them. Hence he was able to act as a brake on some of Lloyd George's wilder schemes. He also kept the backbenchers informed of the Prime Minister's thinking. He was thus an effective mediator between the government's two wings.

Yet this arrangement was not likely to last indefinitely. At times Lloyd George seemed to revel in a political insecurity that gave full scope to his remarkable capacity for improvisation and intrigue, but he soon saw the need for a realignment in British politics. He wanted to form a new centre party and called for the amalgamation ('fusion') of the Lloyd George Liberals with all but the extreme ('diehard') right wing of the Conservative party. There had been over five years of effective co-operation between these groups, and there were many who agreed with former Conservative Prime Minister Arthur Balfour, who wrote in 1918 that 'our party, on the old lines, will never have any future again in this country'. In March 1920, 95 Conservative MPs petitioned for the development of the coalition into 'a single united party'. Lloyd George was keen. A new party, led by himself, would be the answer to his political prayers. But the coalition Liberals – a political rump whose position seemed so vulnerable – foiled his plans. He tried to rally them by insisting that the old parties should combine to resist the common, socialist enemy, but they were unwilling to be tied permanently to the Tories.

Bonar Law described what happened in a letter to Balfour on 24 March:

1 LG first of all met his Liberal ministers and he found that they were much more frightened at the idea of losing their identity as Liberals than he had expected. In consequence when he met the Coalition Liberals as a whole he spoke only of the need for closer co-operation ...

5 Personally I am not sorry at the turn events have taken. I do not like

the idea of complete fusion if it can be avoided, but I had come to think, as you had also, that it was really inevitable if the Coalition were to continue. But it always seemed more important from LG's point of view than from ours. As a Party we were losing nothing and, since the
10 necessity of going slowly has come from LG's own friends, I do not regret it.

Lloyd George was undeterred. He told his secretary (and mistress) Frances Stevenson that he would now use the tactics of the Saracen warriors, who used to sweep down upon their enemy again and again until the time was ripe to drive home their charge. In fact, March 1920 was the closest he ever came to making the coalition permanent. The co-operation achieved in the Commons between the two groups was never matched in the constituencies, and fusion was probably a pipe-dream anyway. Lloyd George's image of defeating a foe was perhaps an unconscious admission that he would have to force an unwilling 'partner' into a new party – an impossible basis for a real political realignment.

The failure of 'fusion' did not mean the end of the coalition, but it did leave Lloyd George vulnerable and dependent on the good works of Bonar Law. Yet in May 1921 Law resigned from the cabinet and the leadership of his party because of ill health, though keeping his seat in the Commons. This was a body-blow to Lloyd George. The *Financial News* predicted it would be 'the beginning of the end of the Coalition Government'. Bonar Law was replaced by Austen Chamberlain.

Chamberlain did not relish his new position as party leader, accepting it only out of a sense of duty. He proved to be no substitute for Bonar Law. He was deficient where Law had excelled – at interpreting the feelings of the Tory backbenchers to the Prime Minister, and *vice versa*. He was out of touch with party feeling, and seemed aloof to a fault. The root of the problem was his vanity. He was short-sighted, but in an attempt to look like his famous father, Joseph Chamberlain, would wear only a monocle. The result was that he often could not recognise even close friends at a distance greater than a few feet. Not surprisingly backbenchers were annoyed at being ignored ('cut' was the popular phrase) by their leader. Nor did the secretive Chamberlain communicate well. He was critical of Lloyd George and thought he should cease to be prime minister after another general election. But he failed even to hint at this to his backbenchers, most of whom thought he was Lloyd George's 'creature'. Asquith compared the coalition under Lloyd George and Austen Chamberlain to a pair of scissors with only one blade. Churchill said of Chamberlain that he 'always played the game – and always lost.'

Had Bonar Law not resigned in 1921, the coalition would probably have had an easier passage over the next few years. But problems were already beginning to multiply, and it is perhaps best to see his resignation as speeding up, rather than actually causing, the downfall of Lloyd George.

3 The Economy and the Failure of Reconstruction

> **KEY ISSUE** How did the postwar slump affect the government's plans for social spending?

The Coalition was elected during a period of high optimism. Indeed there was an excess of optimism: too much was expected too soon, so that disappointment with failure was all the more bitter. Britain was to be transformed into a land fit for heroes. A Ministry of Reconstruction, set up in 1917 under a Liberal minister, Christopher Addison, had developed plans for a housing programme, an extension of unemployment insurance and the abolition of the old poor law. After the election Addison took over as head of a new Ministry of Health, and he, more than anyone, typified the new aspirations – just as his dismissal in July 1921 symbolised the end of reconstruction.

The government is usually described as having failed in the field of social reform. But this charge does not take account of the fact that conditions were very difficult. The basic problem was the effect of the war on the British economy. 745,000 Britons had been killed (9 per cent of all men under 45) – an influenza epidemic killed another 150,000 people in 1918–9 – and 1.6 million had been wounded, many so seriously that they could never work again. In fact about 3.5 million people, including widows and orphans, were soon receiving some form of war pension or allowance. Many markets were lost to Britain during the war and substantial debts were incurred, especially to the United States. Britain was owed more by other countries, especially Russia, than she owed to the USA, but her debtors failed to pay up. In addition, the war had produced over-investment in the staple industries (iron and steel, shipbuilding, coal, textiles) whose products were not needed in such quantities after the armistice. There was in fact a short-term boom at the end of the war, with spiralling inflation. But interest rates were then raised and the boom gave way to depression. The turning point was the winter of 1920–1. In December 1920 unemployment climbed from 300,000 to 700,000. By June 1921 it was over 2 million.

The government's response was predictable, given its political complexion. There could be no complete system of protection against foreign imports on political grounds, given that tariffs were a divisive issue: many Liberals, and indeed some Conservatives, clung to the nineteenth-century policy of free trade. Instead, the government yielded to an 'anti-waste' campaign whose more vigorous supporters seemed to consider almost all government spending to be waste. 'Squandermania' was the charge levelled at the coalition. It was indeed widely believed that in a time of depression government should cut back and spend less; and at the end of 1921 the Chancellor of the Exchequer called on ministers to reduce their budgets by £175 million, out of a total expenditure of £1,136 million. When the departments could agree on cuts of only £75 million, Lloyd George set up a committee chaired by Eric Geddes to find the remaining £100 million. In the end the 'Geddes Axe' pruned only £64 million, but it became the symbol of the government's retrenchment and of the end of reconstruction. The budget of 1922 saw a 12 per cent cut in government spending. Socially valuable scheme, like the planned raising of the school leaving age from 14 to 15, were abandoned. Later governments reached for the axe, as if by a reflex action, during times of depression.

Farmers were major victims of this campaign. The 1920 Agriculture Act had guaranteed minimum prices to producers and when market prices began to fall this involved sizable subsidies. Now the government went back on its word, resulting in hardship and also in the alienation of between 40 and 50 MPs who represented rural constituencies.

The main casualty of the cuts, however, was reconstruction, an area in which the government was thought to have failed despite extravagant spending. Yet the reforming record of the government seems a good one in retrospect and in comparison with later efforts. The 1920 Unemployment Insurance Act extended the existing scheme to cover almost all workers earning less than £250 a year, of whom there were about 12 million, though agricultural labourers and domestic servants were excluded. Insured men could claim benefit of 15s (75p) a week and women 12s (60p) for a maximum of 15 weeks in any one year. In 1921 the act was extended to provide 'uncovenanted benefit' ('the dole') for those who were not insured or whose 15 weeks of benefit had expired, although it would only go to those 'genuinely seeking work'. Benefit could now be paid for two periods of 16 weeks. There were also extra payments available for dependants: 5s (25p) for a wife and 1s (5p) for each child, up to a maximum of four. Pensions were also increased. These were important measures, even though poor law charity was still needed by many families. It has been argued, perhaps somewhat melodramatically, that these reforms averted revolution in Britain.

Housing was Addison's prime interest. Estimating that there were 400,000 houses in Britain unfit for human habitation, he set up a system in 1919 whereby 11 regional commissioners encouraged local authorities to build new houses subsidised by the central government. Cash would be provided by the Exchequer to make good the difference between the cost of building a house and the amount it could raise in rent. The government also made it easier for local councils to

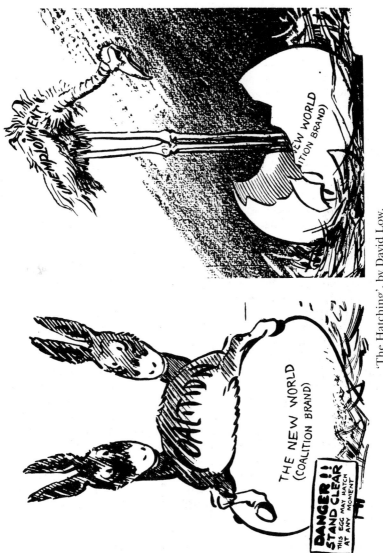

'The Hatching', by David Low.

demolish slums and to acquire building land. But there turned out to be more problems than expected. Local authorities were reluctant to act, bricklayers were in shorter supply than before the war, and builders opted for more profitable construction tasks. In these circumstances Addison did as well as he could. By July 1921 100,000 subsidised houses had been built, and in total 170,000 were erected during the life of the government.

The housing programme was a qualified success. But of course it did not live up to people's hopes or expectations (see Low's cartoon, 'The Hatching', on page 23). 'Homes fit for heroes' were now referred to as 'homes only heroes would agree to live in'. To the anti-wasters, Addison had spent too much too recklessly. Under his scheme, they said truthfully but unfairly, houses had been built for £910 each whereas a few years later they cost only £385. Addison had indeed been unable to look into the future and predict a rapid fall in prices during the slump. In July 1921 he resigned from the government when house subsidies were limited, so that even existing contracts could not be honoured. After the Geddes Axe they were stopped altogether. Addison's defeat seemed total. But in fact, as well as being responsible for building a substantial number of houses, he had done much to ensure that in future housing needs were looked upon as a government responsibility instead of being left to market forces. The Housing Acts of 1923 and 1924 followed the example he had set.

a) Industrial relations

The government's record on reconstruction was one of relative success (and therefore, by definition, of relative failure). The same may be said of its policies in the field of industrial relations, and in each case the key factor in producing success or failure was the performance of the economy. There was a new militancy among the trade unions after the war. Some said this stemmed from the success of the Bolshevik revolution, and indeed red revolution was feared in Britain for a time. In January 1919 70,000 workers came out on strike in Glasgow for a shorter working week. The red flag was raised from the town hall and crowds were baton-charged by police. A deteriorating situation led the government to send in troops, lorries and tanks. Troops were also used on several later occasions, but this was the most menacing incident between 1918 and 1922. The government has been criticised for its heavy-handed tactics, as have workers' leaders for their essentially political motivation; but the situation was soon calmed and a compromise reached.

Lloyd George earned the anger of the organised trade union movement by refusing to nationalise the coal mines. In 1919 he had set up the Sankey Commission to head off a national miners' strike, but he refused to accept its recommendation – agreed by the narrowest of margins, the casting vote of the chairman – in favour of nation-alisation. The mine owners had made a bad impression on the com-missioners: one of them had even said that coal dust was good for miners' lungs! But the Tory backbenchers really gave Lloyd George no choice. Nationalisation was not politically practical; and so the mines, like the railways, were returned to private ownership. Already the post-war period had been marked by a number of strikes, even among the police. Now, partly out of a sense of betrayal, strikes increased in frequency and duration. In 1921 almost 86 million work-ing days were lost, over twice as many as in any year this century before the General Strike of 1926. This seems a poor record, but it should be seen against a background of even more bitter industrial conflict in Europe where industrial turmoil and general strikes took place in France, Italy and Germany.

A general strike seemed certain in Britain in April 1921, when the 'triple alliance' of railwaymen, miners and transport workers threat-ened common action. The Prime Minister intervened personally and negotiated with union leaders. He managed to isolate the miners' fed-eration, so splitting the alliance. When a strike did take place it involved the miners alone. By 1922, when recession had blunted union militancy, the number of days lost was below 20 million. It has been argued with some justification that the government did reason-ably well between 1918 and 1922. Violence was at a minimum, national cohesion was not lost, and at least the door of 10 Downing Street was always open to union leaders.

4 The Irish Question

> **KEY ISSUE** How was the Irish settlement of 1922 brought about and what were its consequences?

Easily the most troublesome political problem that faced the coalition was Ireland – or rather, the conflicting and seemingly irreconcilable claims of Irish nationalists, who wanted independence for Ireland, and unionists, who wished to maintain the union with Britain.

The historical roots of the problem lay in the sixteenth century, when Tudor monarchs tried to pacify Ireland by implanting 'reliable' English, Scots and Welsh subjects on land confiscated from Irish rebels. This process was intensified in the seventeenth century, when the Irish backed the 'losers' in the great upheavals of those times, Charles I and then James II. What made matters far worse was that this time the new landowners were protestant. At the start of the sev-enteenth century, 90 per cent of Irish land was owned by catholics; by the end of the century 85 per cent was in protestant hands. The new settlers were especially numerous in the province of Ulster in the north. This was soon to become Ireland's most industrially prosperous region. Geographical, cultural, religious and economic differences produced two communities in Ireland with separate national identities. This was the basis of the complex Irish question.

An Irish Home Rule movement became active in the mid--nineteenth century and achieved major political support when Prime Minister Gladstone was converted to its cause. However, his Home Rule bills of 1886 and 1893 were defeated and gradually more radical activists came to dominate Irish politics. Before the first world war moderate Home Rulers remained in the majority, but slowly the initiative began to pass to Sinn Fein ('Ourselves Alone'), a republican party founded in 1905 and calling not for local self-government but for independence from Britain. Ranged against them were the Irish opponents of Home Rule and independence. They formed themselves into a unionist movement and gained support from influential British politicians, especially Conservatives, campaigning under such slogans as 'Ulster will fight, and Ulster will be right'. Radicalism soon produced militarism. In 1912 100,000 'loyalists' formed the Ulster Volunteer Force (complete with a £1 million indemnity fund for the support of future widows and orphans) and the nationalists responded with the Irish Volunteers.

Bonar Law, the Conservative leader from 1911, supported the unionists. Many Tories believed that the loss of Ireland would encourage nationalists elsewhere, including those in India, and would eventually lead to the break-up of the whole British Empire. They regarded Ireland as an integral part of Great Britain and insisted that Ireland was prospering (as indeed Ulster was) and that the southern Irish should not be allowed to overrule the wishes of the British people as a whole. On the other hand, Liberals like Lloyd George tended to be more sympathetic to the nationalist cause. They believed that while it would be wrong to force self-government on the protestants of Ulster, it would also be wrong to allow this minority to stifle the legitimate aspirations of the majority of the Irish people. Complex moral issues were involved – and politically explosive ones.

In 1914 the situation was fluid. It was possible that a federal structure might be adopted for the whole of the United Kingdom, so that there would be several regional parliaments, or that Ulster (or those areas of Ulster with a majority of protestants) might be allowed to contract out of the jurisdiction of an Irish parliament. But the war was no time for political experiments; and when the Easter Rising of Irish nationalists took place in Dublin in April 1916, the British authorities reacted strongly. Many Irish catholics had volunteered to fight for Britain against Germany, and the Rising was in fact the work of only a small number of people. Only a minority saw Britain's danger as Ireland's opportunity. But now the British created martyrs. One of the rebel leaders, Eamonn de Valera, was sentenced to death but was not executed because he held a United States passport. Fifteen other leaders were shot. There was a wave of revulsion against British rule, kept alive in 1918 by an unsuccessful attempt to impose conscription. A tremendous boost had been given to the nationalist cause. Hence in December 1918 Sinn Fein won 73 out of the 105 Irish seats at Westminster. Half of the successful candidates were in British prisons at the time, and those who were free refused to take their seats in London. Instead Sinn Feiners formed their own parliament, the *Dail Eirann*, at the Mansion House in Dublin and proclaimed the whole of Ireland an independent republic, with de Valera as its first president. Around the same time a nationalist army was set up – the Irish Republican Army (IRA). They simply ignored the 1920 Government of Ireland Act, which proposed the creation of two separate parliaments, for the north and the south, which would be in charge of most internal affairs. This might have formed the basis of a settlement in 1914; but now it seemed too little, too late.

Lloyd George had to grapple with this issue. No solution was immediately apparent, especially given the differing principles and prejudices of the Conservatives and Liberals in his government. The policies he pursued were anything but consistent. First he went along with the Conservative line and attempted to reimpose 'law and order' (i.e. British rule) on the south, aided and abetted by the 'Black and Tans', ex-servicemen who reinforced the Royal Irish Constabulary and tended to be a law unto themselves. What was essentially an Anglo-Irish war had begun. British policy seemed to be to defeat the Irish insurrection by whatever means were necessary. Martial law was formally proclaimed in December 1920, but even before this the Irish Secretary had been given power to imprison without trial. Atrocities were undoubtedly committed by both sides. On 21 November 1920, 'Bloody Sunday', 14 Britons were dragged from Dublin hotels and shot, and that same afternoon, probably as a reprisal, British troops fired on an unarmed crowd at Croke Park in Dublin, killing 12 spectators and wounding 60. The following month much of the city of Cork was burnt by the Black and Tans. Probably almost 1,000 people were killed in Ireland between January 1919 and July 1921.

This violence tarnished Lloyd George's reputation. Although the atrocities in Ireland owed more to the men on the spot than to him, he bore the ultimate responsibility as prime minister and took the blame. Liberal and humanitarian feeling in Britain was outraged. Asquith, who had returned to the Commons in 1920, judged that 'things are being done in Ireland which would disgrace the blackest annals of the lowest despotism in Europe.' He seemed to be speaking for all Liberals, including those in the coalition. A Labour party commission reported similarly: Britain's actions 'must make her name stink in the nostrils of the whole world'. However, the crucial political factor, as ever, was Conservative backbench opinion. Most, but not all, Tories approved the policy of meeting terror with terror.

In July 1921 British policy was reversed, a truce was signed and negotiations replaced violence. No one is completely sure why, and the official papers on this issue are still closed. Certainly the transformation owed something to the intervention of the king, George V. Perhaps the policy of reprisals had all along been intended to 'soften up' Sinn Fein. The republicans had begun to lose the war and probably could not have held out much longer. Now, for the first time, they were willing to negotiate. Lloyd George met de Valera, and in October 1921 other republican leaders, including Michael Collins and Arthur Griffith, came to London for talks. In some ways they were out of their depth with the Prime Minister, who was a brilliant and cunning negotiator.

The nationalists wanted two things most of all – a united Ireland and a republic. They got neither. Lloyd George knew that he had to retain Ulster (or rather the six of Ulster's nine counties with the most protestants) as an integral part of the United Kingdom. This meant that Ireland must be partitioned. The Conservatives, most of whom would have preferred a united Ireland under British rule, insisted on this. Bonar Law even threatened to return to active politics and lead a revolt against the coalition if Ulster were not safeguarded. Lloyd George also offered 'dominion status' rather than independence, again because of Conservative wishes. The exact meaning of dominion status had not been established, but basically it meant complete self-government within the British Empire. Under this system, a new self-governing Ireland would not be a republic, for the British monarch would still be head of state, to whom an oath of allegiance would be due.

Intense, wearying negotiations took place. In the end Lloyd George got his way, but only after threatening a resumption of war – 'and war within three days'. Perhaps he was bluffing: certainly a renewal of violence would have been unpopular with the public, but Griffith and Collins were 'bounced' into accepting. On 6 December 1921 they signed the Anglo-Irish Treaty. The *Dail* later ratified the treaty only very narrowly, by 64 votes to 57. De Valera was one of its strongest opponents. There were also bitter debates in the House of Commons, but here the treaty passed more comfortably. The Irish question had not been 'solved': but at least it had been answered, even if the answer did not suit everyone. Given the intricacies of the problem and the constraints on government action, the Prime Minister had succeeded remarkably well.

It has commonly been supposed that the Irish treaty was the major cause of Lloyd George's downfall. Certainly it must have rankled with many Conservatives, who for decades had been committed to retaining the union with the whole of Ireland. Indeed the Conservatives had been widely known as 'Unionists' before 1921. One MP was disgusted that 'the man in power [in Ireland] is the man with the gun'. There was a hard core of around 20 'diehards' resolutely opposed to the settlement. But the great majority of Conservative backbenchers voted for the treaty and, had they not done so, it could not possibly have been passed. The settlement itself did not cause the downfall of Lloyd George. The treaty had been signed in December 1921, and the bill proclaiming the Irish Free State (later renamed Eire) became law in March 1922, whereas Lloyd George did not fall until October 1922. It was the short-term consequences of the treaty, rather than the treaty itself, that harmed him most.

The settlement was hated by many in Ireland to whom partition was unnatural and the oath of allegiance repugnant. A virtual civil war began in the new self-governing state. Michael Collins and many others were killed. This did not cause undue heartache among British Conservatives, but the deaths were not confined to the south. The northern division of the IRA waged a campaign of violence in the six counties of Northern Ireland. In 1922 232 people were killed, about 1,000 were wounded, and property valued at over £3 million was destroyed in the north. On 22 June 1922 the Ulster MP Sir Henry Wilson was assassinated in London. Bonar Law's response was ominous for the Prime Minister. 'I agree with the treaty, but I confess, had I seen what the position would have been today, I doubt whether I would have voted for it.' In the autumn of 1922, just before a 50-year period of stability in Irish affairs, Lloyd George's 'settlement' seemed to have settled nothing. His Irish policy, which we now regard as an outstanding achievement, seemed an obvious and costly failure.

5 Foreign Policy, Scandal and the Fall of Lloyd George

> **KEY ISSUE** How did grievances against Lloyd George combine to bring about his downfall in October 1922?

a) The Versailles Settlement

For the purposes of analysis historians usually divide their material into separate compartments. This makes for order and clarity. It can be misleading, however, for politicians are rarely able to consider issues in such a way, completing one before addressing the next. Certainly foreign policy was a constant concern for Lloyd George and the coalition leaders, and a distraction from their other worries. From January to June 1919 the Prime Minister was in Paris helping to draw up the peace treaties with Germany and the other defeated powers. The famous Treaty of Versailles with Germany bears his imprint, and his was essentially a moderating influence. He insisted, for instance, that a reparations total should not be decided immediately. Instead, a commission was appointed to assess German liability for war damages. It was also due to his influence that plebiscites (votes) were held in Upper Silesia and elsewhere to decide the country to which each area should belong. Yet although present-day historians are likely to see Lloyd George's virtues as a peacemaker, many people at the time saw things differently.

Contemporary opinion was in fact divided. In April 1919, 233 Conservative MPs signed a telegram expressing their fear that the treaty with Germany would be too lenient, and so it was considered by many. Lord Northcliffe's papers, *The Times* and the *Daily Mail*, took this line. Yet liberal opinion soon branded Versailles too harsh. This was the message of Maynard Keynes's brilliant *Economic Consequences of the Peace*, an international bestseller that was translated into nine languages within a year of its publication in 1919. Keynes made it fashionable in intellectual circles to condemn the treaty and Lloyd George's part in it.

Keynes believed that Europe was a single economic unit (it 'throbbed together') and that if Germany were impoverished the whole of Europe would suffer. In fact, Lloyd George believed much the same, and his foreign policy 1919–22 was designed to reconcile France and Germany and – after a brief and unproductive intervention against the Bolsheviks in the Russian civil war – to bring the Soviet Union back into world affairs. One Tory leader insisted that Britain should not parley or trade 'with such a blood-stained villain as Lenin'. Lloyd George did not agree: 'after all, we trade with cannibals in the Solomon Islands'.

The only problem with Lloyd George's policies was that they did not work. After the lengthy Paris peace conference, the Prime Minister attended 23 full-scale international conferences. Contemporaries called them his 'circuses', and one historian has referred to them as 'meaningless gyrations'. He could not overcome French resentment towards the Germans or the problem of United States isolation from world affairs. A conference in Genoa in April 1922, which he hoped would 'restore his star to the zenith' and pave the way for a successful general election, was in fact counter-productive. The only result was a disastrous one: the two outcast nations, Germany and Soviet Russia, met together in a nearby town to sign the treaty of Rapallo.

b) Chanak

Lloyd George's greatest error in foreign policy came with the Chanak incident of 1922, which did much to determine the timing of his fall. He had helped to negotiate the Treaty of Sèvres with Turkey, as a result of which most of the Ottoman Empire had been parcelled out between the victorious powers of the First World War. Britain had been given Palestine and Mesopotamia (Iraq). France, Italy and Greece had also been beneficiaries. In fact, the terms of the settlement had been so harsh that they had helped provoke a nationalist revolt against the sultan. An army officer, Mustapha Kemal, had set up a provisional government and had begun a war of liberation. In particular, he wished to wrest Smyrna from the Greeks (see the map below). Britain, France and Italy decided to back Greece in its stand against Kemal, but they backed a loser. In August 1922 the Turks massacred about 100,000 Greeks in Smyrna. They then pushed on towards the Dardanelles and mainland Europe. Chanak, guarded by allied troops, seemed to be in danger, and when French and Italian detachments were withdrawn, a war seemed possible between Britain and Turkey.

The *Daily Mail*'s headline read 'Get Out of Chanak' – an order addressed to Lloyd George, not to Kemal. But the Prime Minister was determined to stay. The cabinet told the British commander, General Harrington, to present the Turks with an ultimatum to withdraw their forces. To some this seemed needlessly provocative, and fortunately Harrington turned a Nelsonian blind eye to the order. Instead he negotiated and signed a pact with the Turks. This eventually paved the way for an amicable settlement in which Sèvres was replaced by the more moderate Treaty of Lausanne.

Chanak and the Middle East, 1922–3.

Chanak did Lloyd George and the coalition much harm. To begin with, his pro-Greek policy offended the traditional pro-Turk stance of many Conservatives. More importantly, the Prime Minister seemed to be recklessly risking war at a time of general war-weariness in Britain. Conservative opinion – and perhaps even public opinion – was summed up in a letter Bonar Law wrote to *The Times*: 'We cannot act alone as policeman of the world.'

c) The Honours Scandal

The Chanak incident occurred at a crucial time. The Irish settlement appeared to be collapsing, and now a scandal erupted which seemed to show the moral bankruptcy of the Lloyd George regime. He was accused of selling knighthoods and peerages. The Prime Minister had never enjoyed a reputation for orthodoxy or absolute honesty. His use of the 'garden suburb' seemed to undermine the civil service, and some said he was in effect introducing a presidential style of government in place of Britain's traditional cabinet system, under which a prime minister was merely the 'first among equals'. In September 1921 he summoned a cabinet meeting in Inverness town hall to suit the convenience of his holiday in the Scottish Highlands. Chamberlain considered this 'outrageous' and all the ministers were annoyed. Lloyd George seldom visited the Commons, he leaked secret information to the press, and there were well-founded rumours that his private life was not above reproach. 'The Goat' had a wife and also a mistress, and it was said that he was unfaithful to both of them. Much was known at Westminster of his scandalous conduct, and more was suspected. A good deal could be read into a remark of Bonar Law's, that if he spoke freely for five minutes, Lloyd George would have to retire from public life. The Tories – if not more moral than others, then certainly more moralistic – seemed to be appalled. Now charges of financial corruption were levelled at the Prime Minister as well. It was said that in order to establish a personal political fund he was virtually selling honours. Handsome donations to party funds had in the past frequently resulted in the granting of honours – but usually only after a decent interval had elapsed and providing the recipients had good reputations. Now Lloyd George dispensed with such formalities.

The Conservatives were perhaps guilty of double standards. They pocketed half the money Lloyd George raised and then complained. But certainly there was much to complain about. It was joked that one client had signed a cheque in payment for a peerage with the title he proposed to take, thus ensuring there could be no double-dealing. In July 1922 it was announced that peerages were to be conferred on three particularly disreputable characters (Sir J.B. Robinson, Sir Samuel Waring and Sir Archibald Williamson). Lloyd George survived a critical debate in the House of Commons but had to accept that henceforth political candidates for honours should be subject to a committee of privy councillors.

d) Lloyd George's Fall

Chanak, coming on top of such scandal, was to many the last straw. Lloyd George seemed to be whipping up a war scare in order to create the right atmosphere for a successful election. A close friend urged Austen Chamberlain against 'undue loyalty' to the Prime Minister, but Chamberlain ignored the advice. He called a party meeting at the Carlton Club on 19 October 1922 and lectured his backbenchers. He insisted that the Conservatives must maintain the coalition as they could not win the next election without it. His case was unconvincing – especially since, just before the meeting, an independent Conservative had won a by-election at Newport despite warnings that a fight between a Tory and a coalition Liberal would split the vote and let the socialist candidate in. Nor did the inept Chamberlain make it clear that he wished to see a reconstituted coalition after a general election, without Lloyd George as prime minister.

Stanley Baldwin made a most impressive speech. A minister had just described Lloyd George as a 'dynamic force', and Baldwin seized the phrase:

1 I accept those words. He is a dynamic force, and it is from that very fact that our troubles, in my opinion, arise. A dynamic force is a very terrible thing; it may crush you but it is not necessarily right.

    It is owing to that dynamic force, and that remarkable personality,
5 that the Liberal party, to which he formerly belonged, has been smashed to pieces; and it is my firm conviction that, in time, the same thing will happen to our party ...

    I would like to give you just one illustration to show what I mean by the disintegrating influence of a dynamic force. Take Mr Chamberlain
10 and myself ... We stand here today, he prepared to go into the wilderness if he should be compelled to forsake the prime minister, and I prepared to go into the wilderness if I should be compelled to stay with him.

The speech probably had no great influence on Tory MPs, but it expressed simply and clearly what many of them were thinking. It also tells us much about the dominant figure in inter-war politics – Baldwin himself.

The next to speak was Bonar Law. Lloyd George's former partner was now his political enemy, but his tone was more moderate than Baldwin's.

1 I saw with perfect equanimity the smashing of the Liberal party; it did not disturb me a bit. As to Mr Lloyd George, whoever else may speak with disrespect of him I never will. We may differ from him, and during the whole course of my co-operation with him I could see quite plainly

5 that the time might come when we would differ; but that difference will
   never make me think that he did not render a service to this country in
   the war for which the country can never sufficiently thank him
   [applause]. Mr Lloyd George cannot look on the Unionist party with the
   same sort of feeling I have. In the nature of the case, although I am sure
10 he does not deliberately try to do it (I am quite sure of that), if it were
   broken I do not think it would break his heart [laughter].

Bonar Law's presence was vital, for he was the figurehead needed to
rally the discontented majority in the Conservative party. A motion in
favour of the Tories fighting the next election on their own was
passed by a large majority, 187 to 87. Chamberlain resigned at once
as party leader. Later that afternoon Lloyd George, after nearly 17
continuous years in cabinet, resigned as premier.

Discontent with the Coalition was unmistakable at the Carlton
Club, but it would be wrong to suppose that all 187 MPs who voted
against continuing the government did so for the same reasons.
Some, such as Baldwin, were motivated primarily by dislike of Lloyd
George's style of government, which seemed to them corrupt. The
'diehards' had been alienated by the softness of Versailles and
appalled by the Irish settlement. Between 40 and 50 MPs for rural
constituencies were motivated primarily by the falling price of wheat.
Many more disliked Lloyd George's policy at Chanak and felt that he
was no longer an electoral asset. The slump, high interest rates, high
unemployment, violence in Ireland – all these meant that Lloyd
George was no longer a vote-winner. Instead he had become a scapegoat for the failure of policies which the Tories had insisted he adopt.

There was, however, a more fundamental reason for the fall of the
coalition. Class conflict had been intensified since the war: workers
saw the dole as miserly and the middle classes saw taxation as excessive. In short, the idea of an all-party coalition no longer seemed realistic. Consensus politics demanded consensus, and this no longer
existed.

6 Conclusion

> **KEY ISSUE** What verdicts can we reach on the Lloyd George
> coalition?

The Lloyd George coalition has been heavily criticised. Asquith called
the 1918–22 parliament the worst he had ever known, and a Labour
MP called it the wickedest. Eric Geddes said that members of the government 'lost all sense of proportion'. A peer, Lord Grey, judged that
the government 'let down and corrupted public life at home and
destroyed our credit abroad'. Today such charges seem exaggerated.

Certainly the government failed to fulfil its election promises, but then conditions in Britain after the war were not conducive to such reforms. The First World War had winners and losers, but at a deeper level all the European participants in this war were losers. All suffered greatly and bore the scars for many years to come. It is tempting to draw a sharp distinction between the successes of the coalition in war and its failures thereafter. But such an argument is superficial. There were far more achievements to the credit of the government after 1918 than is generally admitted – in the fields of reconstruction, industrial relations, Ireland and foreign policy. It is also much more difficult to distinguish between success and failure in peacetime politics (where problems are sometimes insoluble) than in wartime (where there are at least formal winners and losers).

The question of why Lloyd George fell is often asked. There is no easy answer because it is a complex issue involving many factors: his insecure political base, the sheer magnitude of the problems that faced him and the particular policies he pursued. Probably no two historians would agree on the relative importance to be assigned to each of the causes, and most would want to stress their cumulative significance. Perhaps we should consider not why Lloyd George fell, but why he and the coalition lasted so long. He fell in October 1922, but he survived longer than any of the other allied leaders – Orlando in Italy, Clemenceau in France, Woodrow Wilson in America. Similarly we ought sometimes to ask not 'why did the government fail?' but 'how did it manage to achieve so much?'

The other key historical issue for these years is the role and personality of Lloyd George himself. The subject of numerous biographies, he remains a fascinating but enigmatic figure, impossible to pigeon-hole. He was never absorbed by the 'establishment' and was always an individualist and something of a rebel. Mowat has described him as 'a genius with a double dose of everything, good and bad'. In particular, writers have been inclined to exaggerate his qualities and, as a result, to distort our understanding of him. To the socialist intellectual Beatrice Webb he was 'an actor-conjurer'. To the economist Maynard Keynes, a man with a poetic turn of phrase, he was 'this goat-footed bard, this half-human visitor to our age from the hag-ridden, magic and enchanted woods of Celtic antiquity'. He had 'six or seven senses not available to ordinary men' and could understand what others were thinking and were about to say next. And yet, continued Keynes, Lloyd George was 'rooted in nothing': he had no consistent political philosophy or set of principles. He merely wanted to do a deal that would 'pass muster for a week'.

Lloyd George has been depicted as the Goat, the Big Beast, the Welsh Wizard, a Rogue Elephant, a Vampire and a Medium. One might be forgiven for forgetting that he was in fact merely a human being, a man determined to get things done, a man of unfailing zest, impatient of protocol, a man of action who by 1922 was out of touch with public opinion and out of sympathy with the party allegiances that were to dominate the next period in British political history. Lloyd George was a poor party man: a lifelong Liberal (of his own peculiar type), he headed a basically Conservative administration and several times expressed the wish that he had joined the Labour party.

'I am sorry that he is going,' wrote George V in his diary; 'but some day he will be prime minister again.' The king was quite wrong. Lloyd George remained in parliament until his death in 1945 but never again was he to be a member of any government. The age of Lloyd George was over. The high hopes were put aside. People wanted a quiet life, a return to the 'good old days'. Such a thought would have seemed almost blasphemous in 1918, but in 1922 it was commonplace. 'Back to 1914' was a popular slogan. Politics would never be quite as full, as frenzied, as thrilling or as disappointing again.

Summary Diagram
The Lloyd George Coalition, 1916–22

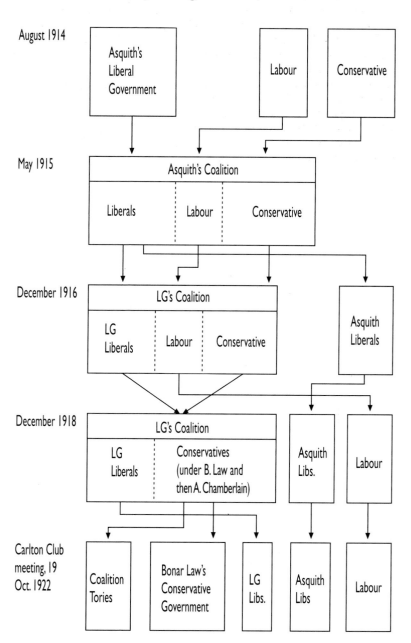

Working on Chapter 2

You will need to make notes on the important political developments – in terms of events, policies and changing personnel – that occurred during and after the war. They should centre on the role of Lloyd George himself and on the reasons for his downfall in 1922. The headings and sub-headings in the text should help you to organise your notes.

Answering structured and essay questions on Chapter 2

Much occurred in the period 1916–22, and as a result a wide variety of questions may be set. It is therefore worthwhile preparing this topic thoroughly.

A typical structured question is

a) What did Lloyd George and his ministers hope to achieve in the field of reconstruction after 1918? (*5 marks*)
b) What social reforms were passed by the Lloyd George coalition? (*5 marks*)
c) Why did the coalition not have greater success in this area? (*10 marks*)

The key to success with all history questions is to answer the question, the whole question and nothing but the question – but with structured or stepped questions you also have to allot your time in accordance with the mark scheme. Hence you must avoid the temptation to spend a disproportionate amount of time on low-mark issues. For the above, you should have little trouble with parts a) and b). These require factual answers, and you should record the relevant facts without time-consuming embellishment. Do not, for instance, set the scene or try to produce polished prose. Just give the relevant information as clearly as possible. Part c), which contains the most marks, requires much more thought. It builds directly on the earlier two parts, in answer to which you will have noted the disparity between the coalition's hopes and achievements. But now you must explain, rather than merely give information. (This part of the question tests *understanding*, which will grow from your engagement with the topic.) Were the hopes of 1918 naïve in any way? Is the explanation basically economic, as the effects of the long world war made themselves felt? How important was the composition of the coalition government, containing far more Conservatives, wary of high government spending in peacetime, than reforming Liberals?

Most essay questions centre on either the war or the post-war years. A typical example of a question on the war years is:

1. What special qualities did Lloyd George bring to the premiership in

1916, and in what ways did he contribute to Britain's eventual success in the First World War?

This is a straightforward question. It is worthwhile paying particular attention to your first paragraph, as the opening section is in many ways the key to a successful essay. It is certainly the first opportunity for you to impress (or depress!) an examiner. There is no perfect way of composing a first paragraph, but there are certain things you ought to be trying to do:

a) You should be explaining the meaning of the precise question set. This involves defining the most important terms in the title and also identifying the periods of time which are relevant. These are vital issues. If you understand the question you are well on the way to answering it, and you will avoid the most obvious fault that can be committed – answering a different question from the one set and thus being irrelevant.

b) You should also be identifying the key areas within the question that need to be addressed in more detail later in the essay. Ask yourself how the question is best broken down into manageable sections. Your practice with structured questions should help you to do this.

c) Finally, you should begin to formulate an argument. You might put forward alternative ideas or you might state your hypothesis. But it is important to begin the argument. Remember that you should answer a question right from the beginning of an essay, and that you should do so directly and explicitly. It is a waste of time and space simply to say that you are going to answer the question. Better to get on and do it, rather than voice good intentions.

You might also think of a 'bold' or 'eye-catching' opening sentence, though this is not absolutely necessary.

A good first paragraph then 'leads in' to the rest of an essay, having analysed the question and outlined an argument. A poor first paragraph often reveals that a student has missed the point of a question. Avoid spending too long 'setting the scene' in a general way, giving background information which is not asked for and which all too often leads into a narrative, which by its very nature tells a story and cannot answer the sort of analytical questions normally set in exams.

Now try to write a first paragraph for the essay question above. Can you think of a good opening sentence? (An observation quoted in this chapter would make a very good, and dramatic, beginning.) Make sure you clarify the period of time relevant to the question and the issues that are relevant. Are there any key terms that need to be defined? Which of his 'qualities' and 'contributions' will you draw attention to in this paragraph, to be dealt with in detail later in the essay? What overall argument might you put forward? This might revolve around the issue of how important his role was in winning the war

A typical question relating to 1918–22 is:

2. Account for Lloyd George's fall from office in 1922.

Variants of this question often appear. In fact it is probably the most popular examination issue for the immediate post-war years. Again it is very worthwhile constructing a first paragraph. Be certain to establish what the downfall consisted of. Only if you are clear what you are trying to explain can you hope to explain it! Which areas will you highlight in the paragraph, apart from the 'obvious' ones such as Ireland, the depression and the failure of reconstruction, the honours scandal, and Chanak and foreign policy failures? You might classify the causes of his downfall into 'pre-conditions', 'precipitants' and 'triggers', or some other system with which you are familiar. Then go on to plan out the rest of the essay in outline. Remember that a good first paragraph is the key to an essay: it should not be a scene-setting exercise that can be detached. Rather than using a narrative approach, gradually working towards Lloyd George's downfall, it is much better to start with the downfall and then look back over the previous years to explain it. After all, in an exam you may run out of time and never reach October 1922!

Questions can cover particular issues, such as the Irish problems, or can cover the whole of the 1916–22 period. A good example of the latter type is:

3. 'He overcame the problems of wartime; but the problems of post-war Britain overcame him.' Discuss this view of Lloyd George as prime minister between 1916 and 1922.

There is probably a natural temptation to agree with a quotation given in such a question. Students probably imagine that only eminent authorities are quoted in essay titles, but this is not always the case. Often examiners make up such quotations, and sometimes they give highly controversial viewpoints which are designed to challenge students. Clearly a good answer to this question must involve identifying the problems Lloyd George faced, together with the policies he adopted and their success or failure. It is worth spending some time trying to identify the range of possible arguments. Try a 'brainstorming' session, identifying as many arguments as possible, and then sort out the sensible from the insupportable.

Source-based questions on Chapter 2

1. David Low's cartoon
Study the cartoon on page 23 and answer the following questions:

a) What is the basic 'message' of the cartoon? To whom was it likely to appeal? (5 marks)

b) To what extent does the cartoon accurately reflect the political reality of the government of the time? (*5 marks*)

c) To what extent is the cartoon an accurate reflection on the reality of reconstruction? (*5 marks*)

2. Baldwin and Bonar Law at the Carlton Club

Read the extracts from Baldwin's and Bonar Law's speeches at the Carlton Club on pages 33 and 34, and answer the following questions:

a) Was Baldwin (line 1) implying that i) a 'dynamic force' is *always* a 'terrible thing', and ii) that inertia is preferable to dynamism? (*2 marks*)

b) What does Baldwin imply are the reasons why he and Chamberlain are taking up opposing sides? (*3 marks*)

c) What evidence does the speech contain that Law respected or liked Lloyd George? (*3 marks*)

d) Quote a short extract to support the contention that Law believed that there had been differences of principle between Lloyd George and the Conservatives (Unionists). On what issues might these differences have arisen? (*5 marks*)

e) What does the tone and style of each speech tell us about its author? (*8 marks*)

f) How well do the two speeches together explain the subsequent vote against Lloyd George? (*9 marks*)

3 Three-Party Politics, 1922-9

POINTS TO CONSIDER

This was a crowded political period which saw four general elections and a general strike. You need to understand the key events of these years and to be familiar with the most important politicians. But be sure to keep sight of overall developments, including the decline of the Liberals, the rise of Labour and winning of supremacy by the Conservative party.

KEY DATES

1918 Labour's new constitution, *Labour and the New Social Order*.

1922 (15 Nov.) general election: clear Conservative victory.

1923 Chamberlain's Housing Act; (May) resignation of Bonar Law, Baldwin as prime minister; (6 Dec.) general election: Labour formed minority government under Ramsay MacDonald.

1924 Wheatley's Housing Act; (Feb.) national dock strike; (March) London tram and bus strike; (August) London conference, resulting in Dawes Plan; (Sept.) the Campbell case, resulting in Labour's resignation; (29 Oct.) general election, after Zinoviev letter: comfortable Conservative victory.

1925 Neville Chamberlain introduced compulsory old age and widows' pensions; Austen Chamberlain helped to negotiate the Locarno Treaty; (April) Britain returned to the gold standard ($£1 = \$4.86$); (31 July) Baldwin's subsidy to maintain wage levels of miners.

1926 Central Electricity Board (CEB) set up; British Broadcasting Corporation (BBC) set up; Germany entered the League of Nations; (March) Samuel Report on mining industry; (3-12 May) the General Strike; (Dec.) end of miners' dispute.

1927 Trade Disputes Act.

1928 Representation of the People Act, establishing votes for men and women at 21.

1929 Local Government Act; (30 May) general election: second Labour Government.

1 The Conservative Government of 1922-3

> **KEY ISSUE** Why did the Conservatives not bring about political stability in this period?

a) Bonar Law as Prime Minister

On Lloyd George's resignation at the end of October 1922, the king called on Conservative leader Bonar Law to form a government. It was not easy for him to do so, since most of the leading Tory figures from the coalition (Austen Chamberlain, Balfour, Birkenhead and Horne) refused to participate. Curzon agreed to stay at the Foreign Office, but Bonar Law found it necessary to promote the little-known Stanley Baldwin to the office of Chancellor of the Exchequer and to include seven peers in his 16-man cabinet – a record number in post-war history. It was, Winston Churchill claimed, merely a 'government of the second eleven'.

Preparations were made for an immediate election, which was held on 15 November 1922. The voters could now record their judgement on politics since the end of the war, and in particular on whether they endorsed the ending of Lloyd George's premiership. The dynamic figure of Lloyd George was opposed at the election by Bonar Law with a policy of 'tranquillity and stability both at home and abroad' (more 'a yawn than a policy', insisted LG). One observer decided that the

STANLEY BALDWIN (1867–1947)

-*Profile*-

Brought up in Bewdley, Worcestershire, where his father was a successful iron and steel manufacturer, Baldwin entered the Commons in 1908. He became Financial Secretary to the Treasury in 1917, and from then onwards was only out of office twice, during the two minority Labour governments, until he retired in 1937. He served as prime minister on three occasions, in 1923, 1924–29 and 1935–37. Yet he did not seem an ambitious man, describing himself modestly as 'just a wheel-greaser' and 'a lazy devil by nature'. Thomas Jones, the deputy secretary to the cabinet, described him as 'one-half contemplative and non-political, more preacher than politician'. Certainly he was sincerely religious. He once said that the salvation of England lay not with that five-syllable French derivative 'proletariat' but with four words of one syllable each: 'faith, hope, love and work'. Yet he was undoubtedly a shrewd political operator, forging for himself a unique image as an entirely trustworthy figure, above the partisan political fray.

General Election, 15 November 1922			
Party	**No. of Votes**	**Percentage of total votes**	**Seats**
Conservatives	5,319,664	37	330
Independent Conservatives	222,410	1.5	13
Labour	4,237,769	29.4	142
Lloyd George Liberals	1,320,935	9.2	47
Asquithian Liberals	2,098,732	14.6	41
Other ('prefixless') Liberals	763,315	5.3	28

election provided a choice between 'one man suffering from sleeping sickness and another from St Vitus's dance'. Yet to most commentators the election was a highly confused affair. The *Manchester Guardian* judged that 'Never perhaps has a general election been held where the issues were less clear and the electors received less guidance.' The root of the problem was the disarray of the party system. Candidates used no fewer than 78 different party labels! Small wonder that Bonar Law expected no party to achieve a majority in parliament. But if the election was a complex affair and the exact results hard to quantify, the basic outcome was simple.

It was one of the closest elections on record. Each of the three parties – if the Liberals can be considered to be one party – won approximately a third of the votes. Over 100 MPs had majorities of less than 1,000. Yet the 'first past the post' electoral system distorted the results into a clear victory. Bonar Law had a majority of 77 seats over all the other parties combined.

All now seemed set for the period of stability which the Conservatives had promised. There were favourable beginnings: the 'garden suburb' was abolished and the Minister of Health, Neville Chamberlain, the half-brother of Austen, introduced legislation to encourage local authorities to build more houses. A subsidy (£6 a year for 20 years) would be given by the central government for each new house completed. There was also success in foreign affairs. Curzon substituted the Treaty of Lausanne for the Treaty of Sèvres, which the Turks had hated so much (see page 31).

This promising start was short-lived, however, because if one international problem was being solved, another was erupting. Tension between France and Germany had been acute since the end of the war. The French thought the Versailles settlement had been too lenient, the Germans that it had been too harsh. Now, in January 1923 the French occupied the Ruhr, the industrial heartland of Germany, in order to extract reparations. Britain had not approved the French action and, indeed, soon insisted that it broke international law. Anglo-French relations were distinctly frosty. Nor were relations with the United States good. The divisive issue here was not reparations but war debts. In December 1922 the Chancellor of the Exchequer was given the difficult task of negotiating in Washington for the reduction of British wartime debts. The Americans drove a hard bargain, and in the end Baldwin agreed that Britain would pay back the full amount over 62 years, with interest averaging more than three per cent a year. The Prime Minister was distinctly unhappy with his Chancellor, but in the end he reluctantly accepted the deal.

Despite these difficulties, the main problem facing the government was in fact Bonar Law's health. For some time he had been scarcely able to speak, and in April 1923 cancer of the throat was diagnosed. He resigned the following month. No machinery for electing a successor existed. It was expected that Bonar Law would nominate a successor, and yet he declined to do so; clearly he had little confidence in the leading contenders. George V therefore had a difficult decision to make.

The leading coalition Tories, headed by Austen Chamberlain, still had not rejoined the Conservative fold and so were ineligible. The choice was therefore very limited. Baldwin was Chancellor and therefore a possibility, but he was almost unknown by the public and was thought to have handled the American debt issue badly. The favourite was therefore Lord Curzon. He had been a successful Foreign Secretary since 1919, had been a member of Lloyd George's war cabinet and, before that, Viceroy of India for six years. In 1923 he seemed to be the one figure of stature within a rather mediocre cabinet. Everyone recognised Curzon's intellectual brilliance and capacity for hard work. Yet many had their doubts about him. He seemed arrogant and overbearing, too conscious of his own dignity and too pompous. A well-known rhyme was often quoted about him:

My name is George Nathaniel Curzon,
I am a most superior person,
My cheek is pink, my hair is sleek,
I dine at Blenheim once a week.

Also, he was a peer. Would it still be possible for a prime minister to sit in the House of Lords rather than the Commons? There was no ready answer to this question; but no peer had been prime minister since 1902, and since then the balance of power in parliament had shifted decisively to the Commons.

Curzon had no doubt that he would assume the highest office in the land. After all, his only rival, Baldwin, was a 'man of the utmost insignificance'. Curzon let it be known that he would not be willing to serve in any subordinate capacity and blithely began planning his cabinet. His disappointment was thus acute when he received the news that he had been passed over. We cannot be sure exactly why the king chose Stanley Baldwin, but it does seem that he was influenced by a memorandum which he thought was the work of Bonar Law. In this Baldwin was praised as a man liked by all in the Commons, as typifying the Conservative spirit and as having the same qualities as Bonar Law, 'honesty, simplicity and balance'. Yet the king had been mistaken, for the memo had been written not by the outgoing Prime Minister but by his secretary.

b) Stanley Baldwin as Prime Minister

In normal circumstances Baldwin would almost certainly not have become prime minister. In fact, many commentators thought he did not possess the qualities to be more than a backbencher. Only the split within the Conservative party – and thus the removal of the leading figures – made him a contender for the leadership of his party. Now luck had helped to give him the premiership. As a result, some historians consider that good fortune was the key to his political success. There is considerable truth in this judgement, but it does not provide a complete explanation. Baldwin had, for instance, shown courage in opposing Lloyd George at the Carlton Club meeting. In addition, he had become respected and liked by all sides in the House of Commons, had very few political enemies, and was in tune with public opinion in 1923. Bonar Law had the great advantage of being totally unlike Lloyd George – and Baldwin was even less like Lloyd George than Law had been! Baldwin, who had come to have a total contempt for Lloyd George's corrupt style of government (and even went so far as to deface a photograph of him), once said that he intended to be a prime minister as unlike Lloyd George as possible; and he succeeded brilliantly. As a result, although he lacked Lloyd George's vices, he was also without his virtues – his dynamism, his originality, and his capacity for resolving problems and getting things done.

Baldwin's elevation produced only a minor cabinet reshuffle. Despite earlier threats, Curzon carried on as Foreign Secretary, and the only major change was the appointment of Neville Chamberlain as Chancellor of the Exchequer. But almost before his government could make any impact on the public, Baldwin called a general election. He wished to introduce protection to help relieve unemployment, and his predecessor had promised that this would not be done without consulting the electorate first:

1 That pledge binds me, and in this parliament there will be no fundamental change … and I take these words strictly. I am not a man to play with a pledge … This unemployment problem is the most crucial problem of our country … I can fight it. I am willing to fight it. I cannot fight
5 it without weapons … I have come to the conclusion myself that the only way of fighting this subject is by protecting the home market [loud and continued cheering]. I am not a clever man. I know nothing of political tactics, but I will say this: Having come to that conclusion myself, I felt that the only honest and right thing as the leader of a democratic
10 party was to tell them, at the first opportunity I had, what I thought, and submit it to their judgements. [Cheers.]

It is doubtful whether Baldwin intended an immediate general election, but now it was impossible to avoid one.

The style of the speech was entirely typical of Baldwin. He believed that the rapid extension of the vote in Britain made it essential that electors should be able to trust their leaders, otherwise democracy would certainly fail. Hence he tried to give the impression of being an honest, average sort of person – someone to be trusted, whose word was his bond and who would never indulge in political double-dealing. Yet many were deeply shocked that another election had been called so quickly. Was this the political stability the Tories had promised?

Why did Baldwin believe an election to be necessary? His government had a comfortable majority and several more years in office. Perhaps he was seeking a personal mandate to carry on, and thus to reinforce his dominance of the party. There is also some evidence that he feared Lloyd George was about to issue a call for protection that might even lead Austen Chamberlain and the other rebel Tories to join him in a new centre party. Hence the election may have been Baldwin's way of pre-empting his political enemy ('dishing the Goat'). Or did he genuinely believe that protection against foreign imports would boost domestic consumption of British goods and thus help cure unemployment? Certainly Baldwin cared passionately about the future of British society. He had a genuine concern that Britain should not follow the road of class confrontation predicted by many on the left. As a religious man, he may even have seen himself as selected by providence to heal the wounds left by the war on British society. He realised that unemployment could produce bitter confrontation, yet he was by no means an economist and never explained how protective tariffs would reduce what became known as the 'intractable million' – the million workers (10 per cent of the insured workforce) who were on the dole in 1923. He may have hoped that protection would have beneficial effects – providing his gamble on election victory paid off.

The Conservatives won virtually the same number of votes as the previous year, but they secured significantly fewer seats. This was due mainly to the fact that the Liberals were now united in defence of free trade, with Lloyd George working, somewhat uneasily, under his old enemy Asquith. The position in parliament was thus a complicated

| Party | General election, 6 December 1923 | | Seats |
	No. of Votes	Percentage of total votes	
Conservatives	5,538,824	38.1	258
Labour	4,438,508	30.5	191
Liberals	4,311,147	29.6	159

one. The Conservatives were still the largest party, but Baldwin had definitely not received the mandate for protection for which he had called. It was a 'hung' parliament, in that any two parties could out-vote the third. Baldwin could not carry on and soon resigned. The king then called for the leader of the second largest party to try to form an administration. Tory leaders consoled themselves with the thought that the socialists would be too weak to do much damage but not too weak to show their incompetence and thus discredit themselves. The first Labour government was born.

2 The First Labour Government

> **KEY ISSUE** Did Labour show that it was 'fit to govern' in 1924?

a) Background

In 1900 the Labour Representation Committee had been set up, becoming known as the Labour party from 1906. It was a federation – in fact, an uneasy alliance – of trade unions and socialist groups, with the addition of many ex-Liberals. It was also divided on ideological lines. Most Labour intellectuals believed that capitalism was doomed to destruction and that socialism would eventually replace it. A minority thought that this would happen very quickly, as a result of revolution. Far more British socialists thought it would be achieved by evolution – slowly, and with what Sidney Webb called 'the inevitability of gradualness'. Yet the intellectuals were vastly out-numbered in the party by the trade unionists, men concerned not with theory but with practical improvements in the wages and working conditions of their members. The trade unionists were dominant: they provided the money the party needed and sponsored the first Labour MPs. They viewed the Labour party as the political wing of their industrial movement.

The problem with the young Labour party had been that it was a specialised interest group: it represented not the nation, or a cross-section of the nation, but the trade unions, to which less than half of Britain's working population belonged. The result was a certain parochialism in the party, a concern that centred too exclusively on issues of direct relevance to the industrial workers. The first Labour MPs had voted with the Liberals and had seldom bothered to attend debates on issues not directly related to industry. How could such a group aspire to be an opposition party, let alone a government? In fact, Labour often seemed to be as much a trade-union pressure group and an extra-parliamentary crusade as an actual political party.

The war had boosted Labour's fortunes and increased its confidence. Two Labour men had gained cabinet experience, and in 1918

Webb drafted a new constitution for the party, *Labour and the New Social Order*. Now, for the first time, individuals could be members of the party and there could be local constituency branches. Labour also had a more clearly defined position: it would work towards a society based not on competitive struggle but on 'planned cooperation in production'. Clause Four spoke of the need to 'secure for the producers by hand or brain the full fruits of their industry ... upon the basis of the common ownership of the means of production'. In the 1918 election Labour fielded over 360 candidates, compared to fewer than 80 in 1910. The party quickly improved its organisation, at national and local levels, establishing a special women's section and taking over several local and one national newspaper, the *Daily Herald*. Electoral success was swift. The party's popular vote, and its number of seats in parliament, increased in each of the three post-war elections until, in 1924, it was given the opportunity to form a government.

Yet there were still problems for Labour to overcome. The 1918 constitution gave Labour a distinctive identity, but Clause Four meant different things to different people. To some, it was an immediate commitment, while to others it was an aim to be pursued in the very distant future. Labour's 'socialism' may indeed have been merely a sop to the intellectuals to compensate for continued trade union domination. The constitution gave the unions the voting power (via their block votes, based on their membership totals) to dominate Labour's annual conference and so, theoretically, to control party policy. The fundamental question remained: could Labour become a national party capable of functioning as a government? Labour's leader, and the new prime minister, Ramsay MacDonald, was determined to answer this question in the affirmative

b) James Ramsay MacDonald

At this time many people held exaggerated fears of a Labour government. It was thought that Labour might disband Britain's defence forces, liquidate the British empire, purge the civil service of right-wing reactionaries, wage war on the rich, and generally alter the British way of life beyond recognition. It was even believed that people's post office savings would be confiscated, that the Christian religion would be outlawed, and that women would be nationalised, causing free love to became the norm and the family system to disintegrate. Underlying these fears was the notion that Labour was secretly communist. It was perhaps all summed up in a jibe of Churchill's that Labour was 'not fit to govern'. On the other hand, many on Labour's left wing had exaggerated hopes of a Labour administration. They wanted Labour to institute a sharp break with the past, to end inequality, exploitation and injustice.

JAMES RAMSAY MACDONALD (1866–1937)

-Profile-

A man of humble origins, being the illegitimate son of a Scottish seamstress, MacDonald devoted his life to the Labour party and to widening the basis of its support. He wished to attract as many voters as possible. He was secretary of the party from 1900 to 1912. As an MP from 1906, he helped to compensate for the insularity of many of his colleagues by concentrating on imperial and foreign affairs. He wrote two books on India, one of which so impressed an Indian reader that he insisted its author's real name must be 'Ramaswami' rather than 'Ramsay' MacDonald. He lost his seat in the Commons in 1918, largely because he had opposed Britain's entry into the war, but he returned in 1922 and was elected leader of the parliamentary party. In 1924 he was the first prime minister from any party to lack ministerial experience. He served again as Labour premier in 1929–31, while from 1931 to 1935 he was prime minister of the National government.

As an orator he was passionate and rousing, but as a manager of men he was too aloof and suspicious. One observer pointed out a contrast in him: 'MacDonald, on the platform, can stir the whole gamut of emotions; meet him and he is as secret as an oyster.' As a result, Beatrice Webb summed him up as 'a magnificent substitute for a leader'. It was partly this aloofness which explains why he formed a coalition without Labour party approval in 1931. He was then promptly expelled from the party.

MacDonald had little sympathy with his left wing. Nor did he have a high opinion of the bulk of trade-union-sponsored MPs. He wished to make Labour a 'respectable' party which drew support from all classes of the community – from 'progressives' as well as from trade unionists and socialists. (Hence he called not for definitely 'socialist' policies but for more vaguely 'socialistic ones'.) He recognised that this could not be done unless the parochialism of the trade unionists was overcome and the left was effectively tamed. In 1924 he had his opportunity. Conditions seemed enormously difficult for him. After all, Labour did not have a parliamentary majority and was not even the largest single party. It was in office but not in power. But, in fact, these conditions proved ideal. The lack of a majority meant he could quite easily resist demands from the left and concentrate instead on administering the system and gaining valuable experience. In consequence he hoped to dispel the irrational fears that many people entertained and to show that Labour was indeed 'fit to govern', thereby broadening the party's appeal. More votes and more seats would be won, and in the fullness of time – when Labour had an overall majority – important reforms could be introduced.

MacDonald chose a cabinet that would help him achieve these aims. He himself became Foreign Secretary as well as Prime Minister. The experienced and popular Arthur Henderson became Home Secretary. Philip Snowden, a rather dour teetotaller who had been crippled in a cycling accident, became Chancellor of the Exchequer. An orthodox financier of the old school, who believed that borrowing was evil, he was a reassurance to the 'city' that there would be no real changes in the financial system. The function of a Chancellor, he once said, 'is to resist all demands for expenditure made by his colleagues and, when he can no longer resist, to limit the concessions to the barest point of acceptance.' The former railwaymen's leader, J.H. Thomas, became Colonial Secretary. He knew very little about the empire, and it was said that he thought 'Uganda' was a term of abuse rather than an East African protectorate. Clydeside MP, John Wheatley, was included as Minister of Health, but he was a token left-winger. The presence of former Liberals and Conservatives and of eight ministers who had been to prestigious public schools underlined the fact that this would be no revolutionary government.

Some historians believe that MacDonald was incompetent and insensitive in his cabinet-making. Others have speculated that he may have deliberately given offices to those unsuited to them, so that ministers would take time to 'learn the ropes' and not interfere unduly with the work of their civil servants. This was certainly the result, if not the intention, of his appointments. After two months in office, MacDonald noted that 'officials dominate ministers. Details are overwhelming and ministers have no time to work out policy with officials as servants; they are immersed in pressing business with officials as masters'.

c) The Work of the Government

Labour's administration did not seem markedly different from that of its Liberal and Conservative predecessors. The empire was safe in Labour hands: colonial rule continued much as before, and the Viceroy of India still made full use of his power to imprison nationalist troublemakers. Not only were the armed forces not disbanded, but five new cruisers were planned and the RAF continued its bombing raids on rebels in Iraq. Procedure in parliament and cabinet followed time-honoured rituals, the only innovation being that smoking was now permitted in cabinet. There were some reforms in social services, but only of a minor nature. Old age pensions were raised, and so was unemployment benefit, and now there need be no gap between the two periods of 16 weeks in any year in which benefit could be claimed. State scholarships to the universities were also revived, undoing the Geddes economies of 1922. But the extra spending involved was small. Snowden saw to that. As a result, there was no serious attempt to grapple with the problem of unemployment. The government simply hoped for a 'revival of trade'. Nor was the Labour government the pawn of the trade unions. Industrial relations were poor, and strikers did not receive favourable treatment. In February 1924 there was a national dock strike for higher wages which ended in success for the workers, but MacDonald had been planning to use troops to unload ships had it continued. The following month he proclaimed a state of emergency during a London tram and bus strike.

As Minister of Health, Wheatley was much more successful than MacDonald had predicted. He was soon spoken of by civil servants as an even more competent minister than Neville Chamberlain. Certainly his Housing Act was the most important legislative achievement of the first Labour government. Chamberlain's subsidy was increased by 50 per cent, from £6 to £9 for each house the local authorities built, and in future it was to be paid for 40 years rather than 20. Wheatley had correctly recognised that the housing shortage was a long-term problem. He also insisted that the houses so subsidised should be for rent rather than for sale, and so the reform benefited the working rather than the middle class. Under the scheme more than half a million houses were built before grants were stopped in 1933.

Further success came in foreign affairs. In many ways MacDonald was fortunate, for post-war tensions in Europe had by now begun to ease. In particular, the occupation of the Ruhr had had a sobering effect on both sides. Initially, the Germans had responded to the 'invasion' by calling for passive resistance in the Ruhr, but its policy of printing money to compensate strikers had fuelled a disastrous runaway inflation. Gustav Stresemann, who became Chancellor in August 1923, soon took the decision to end resistance. As for the French, their action had brought them much international criticism, and in addition the costs of occupation exceeded the value of the reparations that were extracted. The situation was therefore favourable for Franco-German reconciliation.

MacDonald convened a conference in London in August, as a result of which the Dawes Plan emerged. This scaled down German reparations, instituted a new German currency that cured inflation, and provided for the withdrawal of French troops from the Ruhr. It also established the precedent of lending Germany money to pay off its debts and to put its economic house in order. Both France and Germany accepted the plan, which MacDonald correctly called 'the first really negotiated agreement since the war'. A new era of *détente* seemed to have begun, to which MacDonald had contributed constructively. He had never believed that Germany had deliberately caused the First World War and so seemed ideally equipped to facilitate Germany's reacceptance into international diplomacy. He also helped to give the League of Nations a new prestige by speaking at its assembly in Geneva.

Foreign affairs were MacDonald's speciality, and Labour's success in this area owed much to his expertise. Yet there was one issue in foreign policy which threatened to undo all the good work of the government. Labour had taken the common-sense decision to accord diplomatic recognition to the Soviet Union. But MacDonald also wanted a commercial treaty with Russia, and, after negotiations, it emerged that Russia was to receive a £30 million loan. In return, Britain would be compensated for assets seized in the Bolshevik revolution of 1917. It was easily the most controversial issue in the life of the government and, when the treaty was debated in the Commons, it was likely to lead to the government's fall. Before this could happen, Labour went out of office on a trivial but complex issue, the Campbell case.

d) The Fall of Labour

In September 1924 Labour's Attorney-General decided to withdraw a prosecution against J.R. Campbell, the editor of the left-wing *Workers' Weekly*, for urging troops not to fire on their fellow workers. It seems that Campbell, who had an excellent war record, had only been acting-editor at the time the offending material had been published. The case was therefore unlikely to succeed. But the Conservatives complained that the withdrawal had been politically motivated: Labour was interfering with the course of justice. Asquith then called for the appointment of a committee of enquiry; this would take some time to report and so would allow the government to survive. It was a compromise the Conservatives were prepared to accept, but not MacDonald. He insisted that the government would resign if MPs voted in favour of the enquiry – as a majority did. Asquith said that in his 50 years' experience he had never known a government which had 'so wantonly and unnecessarily committed suicide'. MacDonald certainly handled the issue badly. At one stage he even told MPs, quite wrongly, that he had not been consulted over the withdrawal and had to apologise for misleading the House. By this time, it seems that he wished to leave office.

MacDonald was a compulsive worker. His working day, he wrote in his diary, stretched 'from 7am to 1am, with occasional extras'. Unlike Baldwin, he was poor at delegating tasks to subordinates. There is no doubt that he was very tired after combining the offices of prime minister and foreign secretary for nine months. He had made several mistakes, including the acceptance of financial support from a friend, a wealthy biscuit manufacturer, whom he subsequently recommended for a baronetcy – an inept and foolish move, though not a corrupt one, for his friend's public services merited recognition. But he felt that it was his colleagues who were not up to their jobs. He wrote privately that there were 'a lot of duds' in the parliamentary party. MacDonald had little respect for many Labour ministers and was generally alienated from them. His wife had died in 1911 and he was a lonely man prone to depression. Labour was not a harmonious team under Ramsay MacDonald. His colleagues, for their part, felt that although he was probably the best leader for the party, he certainly was not an ideal one.

The first Labour government ended after only nine months. Yet the spirit in the Labour camp was good. They had soldiered on for a reasonable period of time, gained experience and shown that the party was fit to govern. MacDonald expressed these opinions to the king:

1   They have shown the country that they have the capacity to govern in an equal degree with the other parties in the House ... and, considering their lack of experience, have acquitted themselves with credit in the House of Commons. The Labour government has also shown the
5   country that patriotism is not a monopoly of any single class or party. Finally, they can justly claim that they have left the international situation in a more favourable position than that which they inherited. They have in fact demonstrated that they, no less than any other party, recognize their duties and responsibilities, and have done much to dispel
10 the fantastic and extravagant belief which at one time found expression that they were nothing but a band of irresponsible revolutionaries intent on wreckage and destruction.

They expected to improve their position in parliament at the election that the government's fall precipitated, but they had reckoned without the 'red scare'.

Four days before the poll, in a story with the headline 'Civil War Plot by Socialists', the *Daily Mail* published a letter supposedly written by a leading Bolshevik, Zinoviev, to the Communist Party of Great Britain calling for revolution. The letter was used by Conservative supporters to damn the government. One Tory pamphlet argued that 'there are many Communists today in our so-called "Labour Party"; and so strong are they that even our Socialist government must do their bidding'. The last days of the campaign certainly saw a strong movement to the Conservatives. The owner of the *Daily Mail* judged that he had probably won 100 seats for the Tories. Labour supporters felt that their government had been the victim of an underhand plot trumped up by their capitalist enemies. Many historians now judge that the Zinoviev letter was a forgery. In fact, their case is not proven and we do know that many similar – and genuine – letters were sent from Moscow to other countries. What we can be certain of is that the real electoral victims were the Liberals rather than Labour.

| Party | General Election, 29 October 1924 | | Seats |
	No. of votes	Percentage of total votes	
Conservatives	8,039,598	48.3	419
Labour	5,489,077	33.0	151
Liberals	2,928,747	17.6	40

Labour lost 40 seats but gained more than a million extra votes. Many voters had clearly been impressed by Labour's moderation in office and were immune to the 'red scare'. Labour seemed to be succeeding in moving into the middle ground of British politics. The 'inevitability of gradualness' was still in operation. On the other hand, the scare tactics employed at the election undoubtedly had an effect. The turnout of voters was much higher in 1924 (76 per cent) than in 1923 (70 per cent), and there had been an important shift from Liberal to Conservative. Politics had been polarised, to the disadvantage of the Liberals. Baldwin was back.

3 The Second Baldwin Government, 1924–9

> **KEY ISSUE** How effectively did this Conservative government cope with the problems that beset Britain?

a) Conservative Administration

The knives had been out for Baldwin when he lost the election at the end of 1923. It was probably only the fact that the minority Labour government was unlikely to last long that saved him. The Conservatives realised that it would be unwise to change leaders shortly before another election. But victory in October 1924, with a majority of over 200, made his position secure. He was 56 and probably at the height of his powers. Political commentators now spoke of a 'New Conservatism' that combined efficiency and moral purpose. Baldwin also had the advantage of a full-strength team. He had used the months in opposition to bring the coalition Tories back into the fold. Austen Chamberlain, Balfour and Birkenhead occupied prominent positions in this government, which proved to be the first postwar administration to run its full term.

Baldwin made one other significant, and unusual, appointment. Winston Churchill, until very recently a Liberal, became Chancellor of the Exchequer. Churchill himself was incredulous, and historians have found it difficult to fathom Baldwin's reasoning. He certainly did not choose him for his financial expertise. The probable answer is that the appointment of this free-trader underlined Baldwin's new repudiation of protection. Having burnt his fingers in 1923, he had become very cautious about such an explosive issue. Now Tory 'tranquillity' could finally come to pass. A.J.P. Taylor has written, with heavy sarcasm, that under Baldwin there was to be 'no Protection, no class war; if possible, there was to be nothing at all'. But there was another reason too for the appointment: just as the rebel Tories were no longer available for Lloyd George's new centre party, so Churchill was out of harm's way. Lloyd George was isolated from the other 'hundred horsepower intellects'.

In foreign affairs, relations with the Soviet Union soon deteriorated. Labour's commercial treaty was abandoned, and a few years later diplomatic relations were broken off after a spy scandal. Yet on the whole Austen Chamberlain was a successful foreign secretary. Certainly conditions were favourable. *Détente* in western Europe had already started, and now Chamberlain smoothed its progress. In 1925 he, along with Stresemann for Germany and Briand for France, negotiated the Locarno treaty. By this agreement, France, Germany and Belgium accepted their common frontiers, while Britain and Italy acted as guarantors. The following year the three statesmen each received the Nobel Peace Prize. What seemed remarkable to contemporaries was not just the agreement itself – though few would have dared predict a few years earlier that Germany's contentious western border would be accepted in this manner – but the new spirit of cooperation and harmony in international affairs, the 'Locarno spirit'. Also in 1926 Germany was admitted to the League of Nations, with a permanent seat on the Council. The League was enjoying a golden period of success and respect. All seemed set fair for prolonged peace in Europe.

Of course there was a good measure of wishful thinking, of delusion, in the *détente* of the mid-1920s, and there were still unsolved problems beneath the surface. Many historians have rightly pointed out that Locarno was not such a momentous achievement as contemporaries assumed. Stresemann suggested the deal to distract attention from the fact that Germany had not scaled down its armaments to the levels specified by the Treaty of Versailles. Also, Locarno said nothing about Germany's *eastern* frontiers, and almost all Germans intended sooner or later to recover territory lost to Poland. Nevertheless there was a relaxation of tension in international affairs and, although there were still problems, the omens for the future looked better than they had for several decades.

b) The General Strike

Baldwin was a man of peace and of compromise. He wanted international conciliation and yearned for industrial conciliation at home. In March 1925 he quashed a backbench Tory bill attacking the 'political levy' which trade unionists automatically paid to the Labour party unless they 'contracted out'. The bill would have insisted that union members 'contract in' instead. Baldwin believed that this reform, although justified on its merits, would embitter industrial relations. His aim in life, he said, was 'the binding together of all classes of our people', and his earnest plea was to re-echo an old prayer, 'Give us peace in our time, O Lord.' His words impressed many of his seemingly more talented cabinet colleagues, as well as MPs on the left. Although the 'diehard' wing of the Tories was angry, Baldwin had the moral prestige and the popularity to defy the right. However, his words turned out to be more impressive than his actions. As was once said of an American President, 'he meant well – but meant well feebly'. He wanted industrial harmony: instead he got the general strike of 1926.

The origins of the general strike are complex. They encompass a history of poor working conditions and of bitter industrial relations in the mining industry. (See the companion volume in this series, *Britain: Industrial Relations and the Economy, 1900–39* for a detailed examination of the causes of the strike.) But the strike also had political origins. Baldwin said that he rejected the idea that the government should attempt to control the British economy. Economic problems would be solved by the people themselves (i.e. market forces): 'it is little that the government can do'. Yet his government did not and could not stand aside from economic matters. In particular, Churchill made the fateful decision in April 1925 to return Britain to the gold standard. At the time most people applauded, but it was later called 'the most dramatically disastrous error by a government in modern economic history', and even Churchill later admitted that he had blundered.

The gold standard was the means by which, before the war, the leading countries had regulated international finance. The pound had been valued in terms of a certain quantity of gold of a certain fineness, and hence its value was fixed in relation to the currencies of other states on the gold standard. Nor could such governments simply print money and cause inflation, as paper money had to be backed by gold reserves. In the early-1920s many Britons looked back longingly to the pre-war days of the gold standard, when the British economy had been much stronger. It was hoped that if the gold standard were restored then prosperity would return. The reasoning was of course faulty. The gold standard may have been the symbol of prosperity but it had hardly been the fundamental cause. Returning to the gold standard was a hopeful act of faith. Churchill also made the fundamental error of returning at the pre-war value of sterling. After April 1925 the pound was valued at 4.86 dollars. The unorthodox economist Maynard Keynes wrote a pamphlet, *The Economic Consequences of Mr Churchill*, in which he insisted that the pound was at least 10 per cent overvalued. He believed that as a result British exports would be over-priced and uncompetitive, and that in consequence there would be attempts to cut back on costs, especially wages. Churchill's decision would therefore, quite needlessly, lead to industrial conflict and cuts in the standard of living of many workers. The coal industry, he predicted, would be the scene of immediate strife. Many economists have subsequently debated Keynes's analysis, and some have disagreed with his reasoning. But no one can deny that his predictions were largely borne out by events.

Strikes in British industry had been diminishing since 1921. Even in the mines the situation had improved. But at the end of June 1925 the mine owners announced wage reductions, a longer working day and local (as opposed to national) wage agreements. Not only was the return to the gold standard making British exports of coal more expensive than before, but now, following the French withdrawal, coal from the Ruhr was available again on world markets. The Trade Union Congress (TUC) promised support for the miners, and a general strike seemed certain. Baldwin (in words that seemed to justify Keynes's prediction) insisted that 'all the workers of this country have got to take reductions in wages to help put industry back on its feet'. Indeed many industrialists now began to speak of 'rationalisation', by which they meant wage cuts. The Prime Minister was under pressure from his right wing to stand aside from the dispute; but instead, on 31 July 1925 (dubbed 'Red Friday' by the unions), he gave a £23 million subsidy to maintain existing wage levels while a Royal Commission, under Sir Herbert Samuel, enquired into the whole mining industry. There was a nine months' truce during which the government made effective plans to counter a future general strike. This was in contrast to the unions, who were complacent, believing they had already won a complete victory.

The Samuel Report of March 1926 was a compromise. It called for the reorganisation of the coal industry, better working conditions and no lengthening of the working day – but also for wage reductions. Neither owners nor unions would accept these recommendations, and the government failed to cajole or coerce them into agreement. Lloyd George might have done better. The more stolid Stanley Baldwin simply wrung his hands at the sorry state of affairs. The coal owners put up lock-out notices and the TUC, with some reluctance, called for sympathetic strike action. The General Strike began at one minute to midnight on 3 May. Almost 2 million workers went on strike. But the government contingency plans worked well, the weather was mild and coal stocks were high. Nor was there any shortage of middle-class volunteers to assist troops in maintaining essential services.

Baldwin decided to give Churchill the job of editing the official government paper, the *British Gazette* ('the cleverest thing I ever did – otherwise he'd have wanted to shoot someone'). It was this paper which set out the government's official policy: 'the General Strike is a direct challenge to ordered government'. The government branded the General Strike unconstitutional and insisted on the 'unconditional surrender' of the strikers. On 12 May they had their way: the TUC leaders backed down. The disparity of power between the two sides had been too great for them. In the nine days of the strike the government spent a total of £433 million, while the TUC had spent no more than £4 million and could afford this only with difficulty. They also feared that, if they stayed out, their already dwindling assets might be seized or that revolutionaries might come to the fore. Baldwin insisted that he would ensure a fair deal for returning strikers. In fact, there was considerable victimisation, so that a largely spontaneous brief resumption of the strike occurred. As for the miners, they stayed out till the end of the year, before accepting total defeat – lower wages, longer hours and local agreements.

A general strike had been the last thing that Baldwin wanted, but at least his government had handled it effectively. Now he told the Commons that he was undaunted: he was still a man of reconciliation. 'Before long the angel of peace, with healing in his wings, will be among us again.' Despite these words, he allowed the Tory right wing to gain the ascendancy, and in 1927 the Trade Disputes Act was passed. In many ways this was the measure that Baldwin had successfully deflected before the strike. It attacked the political levy paid to the Labour party: those who wished to pay would in future have to make a point of 'contracting in'. In consequence, Labour party funds were soon to decline by about a quarter. The act also made any future general strike illegal. Baldwin's reputation as a moderate had been seriously damaged. In fact, he was suffering from nervous exhaustion, and on the orders of his wife and a gynaecologist (the only doctor she could find on a Sunday) he was made to take a holiday.

No one comes well out of the General Strike – neither the owners, miners' leaders, TUC, nor the government. But at least Britain returned to normal with surprising ease and the scars left by the strike seemed to heal very quickly. Union leaders henceforth became more moderate, more willing to co-operate and to compromise, as indeed did some employers. There were fewer industrial disputes over the next decade than in the previous one, and it would be wrong to allow the drama of the General Strike to detract from the constructive work of the 1924–9 government. Baldwin's second administration has been called 'a government without a policy'; but it would be truer to describe it (the General Strike aside) as, in Churchill's words, 'a sedate, capable government'.

c) Conservative Reforms

The constructive element was provided by Neville Chamberlain, the Minister of Health, assisted by Churchill at the Exchequer. Chamberlain drew up a list of 25 bills embodying his reforms: 21 of them subsequently became acts of parliament. There were important additions to welfare legislation. In 1925 contributory old age pensions began: in return for higher national insurance contributions, all workers and their wives would receive a pension of 10s (50p) a week at the age of 65. Before this, pensions had been given at 70, but only to those whose incomes fell below certain levels. There were now to be widows' pensions as well. The system of unemployment insurance was also reformed: some benefits were lowered, but in future benefit could be claimed not just for two 16-week periods but indefinitely, providing the claimant was 'genuinely seeking work'.

Chamberlain's most extensive reforms were in the field of local government. This was an area in which, as a former Lord Mayor of Birmingham, he could claim some expertise. The Local Government Act of 1929 gave local authorities extra duties – including additional powers over roads, public health, and maternity and child welfare – so that now they had greater responsibilities than anywhere else in Europe. Finance to pay for these services was also reformed. In future no rates would be paid on agricultural land, and industry and the railways were to be relieved of three-quarters of their rates. It was hoped that this 'de-rating' would make employers more competitive and so willing to take on extra workers. The Exchequer made good local authorities' loss of £24 million in rates and in addition provided another £16 million to cover the extra duties they had taken on. The result of these reforms was that local councils became more active than ever before. But since an increased proportion of their revenue came from Westminster (i.e. from the national taxpayers rather than the local ratepayers), their independence had correspondingly declined. Henceforth they were, to a larger degree, agencies of the central government.

These were substantial measures, even if not particularly eye-catching or dramatic, and it has been said that Neville Chamberlain did more to improve local government 'than any other single man this century'. Baldwin's government sponsored other reforms too, measures which showed that the Conservatives were not committed inflexibly to *laissez-faire* capitalism. In 1926 it set up the Central Electricity Board (CEB), which encouraged the building of a large number of modern, privately owned power stations, and developed an effective power grid to distribute current over the whole country. As a result the efficiency of the electricity industry was enormously boosted in Britain. At the same time the British Broadcasting Company was taken into public ownership, becoming the British Broadcasting *Corporation*. This was another example of the government's recognition of the virtues of public enterprise. In 1928 the franchise was extended to all women aged 21 and over, so that women could vote on exactly the same terms as men. This meant that the electorate increased from 22 to 29 million, and there were now two million more women voters than men. But would the voters, new or old, women or men, decide to continue with Conservative administration? Had Baldwin's second government done enough to earn reelection?

4 The 1929 Election

> **KEY ISSUES** Why did the Liberal party decline? How did the three parties attempt to win the support of the electorate?

a) Liberal Decline

In 1925 Asquith took a seat in the House of Lords. The following year, after a stroke, he resigned as leader of the Liberal party. His old rival Lloyd George, now 63, was thus left in undisputed charge of the party – but of a declining party, with only 40 seats in the Commons. No doubt Asquith blamed Lloyd George – who split the party in 1916 (see page 13) – for the low ebb of the party's fortunes. Yet the decline of the Liberals was a complex historical phenomenon for which no one person or issue is to blame.

Some historians have identified the *real* decline as stemming from the late nineteenth century. In 1886 Joseph Chamberlain – in defiance of Gladstone, who wanted to see Home Rule in Ireland – distanced the unionist Liberals (who favoured the maintenance of the union) from the official party. In the general election of that year Chamberlain's followers won 77 seats, and soon this group drifted into the Conservative fold. Certainly this weakened the Liberal party. Yet the wound was hardly fatal, since in 1906 the Liberals emerged from a long period in opposition to capture 49 per cent of the total vote and to win a landslide victory.

Other historians have focused on the years immediately before the First World War, when the party was divided between traditionalists favouring *laissez-faire* and reformers, like Lloyd George, who were exponents of the 'New Liberalism' of state-sponsored reform. The most extreme exponent of this interpretation was George Dangerfield, in *The Strange Death of Liberal England* (1935). In his view, the party suffered a series of debilitating crises – over Ireland, industrial relations and suffragette militancy – so that by 1913 Liberal England 'was reduced to ashes'. Certainly there were acute problems in this period. The party lost a good deal of electoral support in the general elections of 1910, so that it became dependent upon the votes of Irish nationalist and Labour MPs, and in 1911–14 it lost no fewer than 14 seats at by-elections. Furthermore, its electoral pact with Labour boosted the infant Labour party and sowed dissension in its own ranks. In all likelihood, the Liberals would have lost the next general election, had the Great War not intervened. Yet the Liberals were still a great party of government, and they passed significant legislation, like old age pensions and national insurance, and they also emerged victorious in their battle with the Lords. No one in 1914 had compelling reasons to believe that the party would soon suffer terminal decline. Dangerfield's book enjoyed popularity more for its racy style than the soundness of its analysis.

Perhaps the war years were crucial, and above all the split between Asquith and Lloyd George in December 1916. The Liberal party, Trevor Wilson has written in *The Downfall of the Liberal Party* (1966), was rather like an individual who, after a period of vigorous health, was admittedly suffering signs of illness (with the problems of 1911–14) but then was run over by a 'rampant omnibus'. 'After lingering painfully, he expired.' What killed the patient was clearly not any pre-existing illness but being flattened by the bus. Certainly the war harmed the Liberal party. War necessitated coalition, thus giving the Conservatives a route back to power, and moreover the necessity for state control inevitably widened the rift between those Liberals wedded to old ideas of individual liberty and *laissez-faire* and the 'New Liberals' like Lloyd George. Crisis came in December 1916, when Lloyd George replaced Asquith as Prime Minister, producing a seismic split in the party that was not healed in time for the 1918 general election (see page 16) and so virtually destroyed the old party.

Perhaps the party would have declined anyway: many wealthy businessmen were switching their allegiance to the Conservatives and the working classes were increasingly attracted to Labour. Enthusiasm for Liberal causes seemed to be waning, and certainly constituency Liberal parties found it difficult to sustain their momentum between elections. Liberalism was decaying even faster in the constituencies than at Westminster, while its ideology seemed increasingly irrelevant. Nevertheless the severing of the party certainly accelerated Liberal decline.

Other historians have focused on the post-war rise of the Labour party and the dominance and strength of the Tories, both of which – together with the British 'first past the post' electoral system – pushed the Liberals into the margins of politics. The Liberals had done badly in the elections that followed Lloyd George's resignation as Prime Minister in 1922, and falls in Liberal votes produced a disproportionate loss of seats (see pages 44 and 47). In December 1923 the Liberals were seemingly united under Asquith and they held the balance in the Commons, but MacDonald refused a coalition or even an electoral pact. The Liberals kept Labour in office but gained nothing in return. There almost seemed to be a conspiracy against them. Labour wanted to be the only progressive party in the Commons and the Tories wanted to be the only non-socialist party. Each, therefore, had a vested interest in seeing the Liberals decline and die. The election of 1924, marked by the Zinoviev scare and a decline of Liberal votes and seats, seemed a final blow to Liberal fortunes. With little industrial and no trade union support, the Liberals found it increasingly difficult to make financial ends meet after the war, and three quick elections in 1922–4 all but exhausted their funds. It was clear that the Liberals, who were unable to contest many more than half the parliamentary seats in 1924 – a year that has been called their 'point of no return' – could not possibly form a government, and this realisation further accelerated the decline in their support. Its only hope seemed to be that proportional representation would be accepted; but the other parties refused to throw them this political life-line. The two-party system had re-emerged: but now it was Conservative/Labour, not Conservative/Liberal.

The debate on the decline of the Liberals has continued for decades. Did the Liberals die a natural death, did they commit suicide, or were they murdered by their political enemies? Or was the corpse capable of resuscitation – not so much dead as merely sleeping? Each of these options has been supported by a variety of experts, but most cautious historians believe that the party's decline – not so much an event (i.e. a single occurrence) as a long process – can only be explained by a combination of factors rather than any single cause. In other words, the various interpretations should be seen as complementary approaches, rather than as alternatives. Yet the most sceptical of historians believe that the decline of the Liberals has yet to receive a satisfactory explanation and that an 'open verdict' must be returned.

b) Liberal Economic Radicalism

Around 1925 reports of Lloyd George's political death were greatly exaggerated. The political situation still seemed fluid, and there was life in the 'Old Goat' yet. The Liberals won six by-elections between 1927 and 1929. To start with, Lloyd George provided the cash needed to resuscitate the party, donating £400,000 from his personal political fund. Equally important, he helped to generate new ideas, gathering round him a 'brains trust', including the economist Maynard Keynes, to work out a radical but non-socialist strategy for the next election. The result was the 1929 programme, *We Can Conquer Unemployment.* The Liberals decided they would address the major problem facing Britain, the 'intractable million':

1 The word written today on the hearts of British people, and graven on their minds is *Unemployment*. For eight years, more than a million British workers, able and eager to work, have been denied the opportunity ... What a tragedy of human suffering; what a waste of fine resources; 5 what a bankruptcy of statesmanship ... At the moment, individual enterprise alone cannot restore the situation within a time for which we can wait. The state must therefore lend its aid and, by a deliberate policy of national development, help to set going at full speed the great machine of industry.

Lloyd George put forward a carefully costed scheme of public works, to be paid for initially by loans. £42 million would be spent on main roads, £20 million on ring roads and £37 million on road bridges. New houses would be built, telephones installed and land reclaimed. 600,000 men a year were to be taken off the dole and employed for two years at a cost of £250 million. But they would not be the only ones to benefit, as there would be a 'multiplier effect'. The construction and electricity industries would have extra orders, and the new workers would become taxpayers and consumers, indirectly causing other men to be employed; and in addition improvements in road and rail communications would boost the economy. Soon government revenue from taxation would rise, allowing the original loan to be repaid.

It was an ingenious scheme that has been praised by several historians as far-sighted and constructive. But there were problems, for many people thought it was too good to be true. Could prosperity be generated at no real cost, without even higher taxes? The programme broke many, if not most, of the accepted economic beliefs of the day. Also, could Lloyd George be trusted? Many remembered his broken promises of 1918. Nevertheless, here was a clear challenge to the two-party system. In 1929 the Liberals fielded 513 candidates, compared with 340 at the previous election, and a Liberal government seemed a real possibility.

c) Labour and the Socialist Creed

In 1929 the Labour party was confident. Its first administration was thought to have been a qualified success, and MacDonald's path of respectability was expected to win more moderate voters for Labour. MacDonald had demonstrated his orthodoxy not only during the government of 1924 but in 1925–6, when he had condemned Baldwin's subsidy to the mines as unwarranted interference in the economy and had disapproved of the General Strike. The failure of the strike seemed to justify his stand, and henceforth trade union leaders began to rally behind the Labour party and its aim of achieving reform through parliament rather than by direct confrontation.

In the election campaign Labour attempted to steal the Liberals' clothes: they insisted that they too would build roads and bridges and employ men through public works, but their programme was not costed and not given great prominence. Labour took their stand on the 'socialism' that gave them a distinctive and separate identity. Their policy document, *Labour and the Nation*, was not so much a programme as a statement of general principles. Labour's aim was defined as the reorganisation of industry in the interests of all, resulting eventually in a 'Socialist Commonwealth'. Socialism was:

ı   neither a sentimental aspiration for an impossible Utopia, nor a blind
    movement of revolt against poverty and oppression. It is the practical

recognition of the familiar commonplace that 'morality is in the nature of things', and that men are, in very truth, members of one another. It
5 is a conscious, systematic and unflagging effort to use the weapons forged in the victorious struggle for political democracy to end the capitalist dictatorship in which democracy finds everywhere its most insidious and most relentless foe.

In other words, socialism had visionary appeal, but it was a moderate and, above all, moral creed, based upon the brotherhood of man. Its content and application were left reassuringly vague. One left-winger complained that this statement would give the next Labour government 'a free hand ... to define any programme it pleases'.

d) The Conservatives and 'Safety First'

The Tory strategy in the election was very much Baldwin's own. It is sometimes said that by 1929 the Conservative government had run out of steam: the amount of parliamentary time lavished on the relatively unimportant issue of the revised Anglican prayer book seemed to show this. Hence, it has been argued, the Conservatives, lacking in positive ideas, had no real programme to put before the electorate. They hoped to exploit a new red scare, but when one did not turn up they chose instead, rather unimaginatively, to call for 'Safety First' (without saying what would come second). Recent research has destroyed this myth. The Tories had policies of which they were proud and which they could have used to spearhead their campaign. The Local Government Act, according to one leading industrialist, was 'the biggest legislative reform of the last 50 years', and de-rating too seemed a major achievement. The government was also working on a scheme to absorb British unemployment by promoting development in the empire and on a new system of maternity and child welfare (to attract the new women voters). Yet Baldwin chose not to highlight these policies, but instead to stand on his record.

The Conservative election platform in 1929 was carefully thought out. Baldwin knew that he could not outbid Lloyd George, whom he believed to be cynically promising what he could not deliver. He himself would make a virtue of promising nothing and refusing to indulge in election bribery. Baldwin implied that it was better to have few policies and to make few pledges – and to fulfil them – than to promise rewards that could not possibly materialise. Therefore he put himself forward as an honest and principled politician. 'You trusted me before', he told his audience in his last election speech, 'and I ask you to trust me again.' He was portrayed on thousands of posters as 'The Man you can Trust.' 'Safety First', the slogan the Conservatives chose to sum up their campaign, was not a substitute for a policy, as many imagined at the time and have believed since. It was deliberately chosen to discredit Lloyd George.

The government was confident of victory, although it expected to have a reduced majority. One Tory insisted during the campaign that 'Baldwin is really our chief asset, and it is almost in fact a one man show.' Neville Chamberlain expected victory by more than 50 seats; the government Chief Whip predicted 80. Baldwin said privately that he was 'banking on the decency of the English people' and their capacity for seeing through Lloyd George's claims. But if the Conservatives lost an election in which he had been so prominent, Baldwin would once more be under great pressure to resign as party leader.

e) The Election Results

Lloyd George dominated the election. His proposals allowed a real choice for the electorate: they could opt for his economic radicalism or the economic conservatism of the other two parties. For this reason the election has seemed to some historians the most important of the inter-war period. Many people at the time believed that the basic choice was between 'capitalism' and 'socialism' (the Conservatives and Labour), yet in practice both Conservative and Labour used similar versions of 'Safety First'.

'Safety First' did not work for Baldwin: its appeal was limited because in 1929 few perceived any real threat. The outstanding problem was unemployment, and that would hardly be cured by more of the same. As for the Liberal campaign, it produced a substantial increase in their popular vote, but only a small increase in parliamentary seats. Admittedly, they now held the balance in the Commons, but neither MacDonald nor Baldwin was likely to share power with Lloyd George in a coalition. His great effort had been in vain. Conservatives and Labour could breathe a sigh of relief: the Liberals were dead, even though they would not lie down. Labour was the real victor: it had won more seats than the Tories, although it had received fewer votes. MacDonald now had the opportunity to form a second minority government.

General Election, 30 May 1929			
Party	No. of votes	Percentage of total votes	Seats
Conservatives	8,656,473	38.2	260
Labour	8,389,512	37.1	288
Liberals	5,308,510	23.4	59

Summary Diagram
Three Party Politics, 1922–9

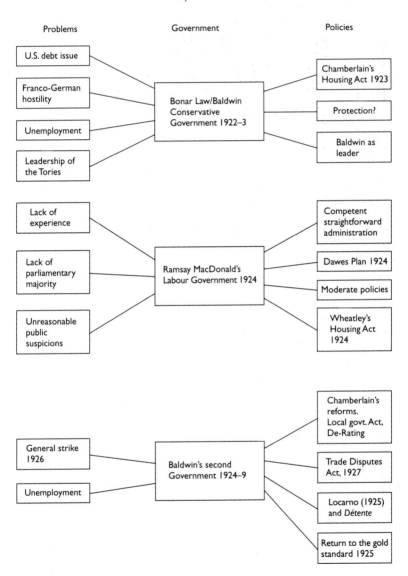

Working on Chapter 3

Your notes on this chapter should provide a summary of the important political developments of the period. Remember that, although
you must understand the chronological course of events, you will
rarely have to give a narrative in the essays you write – and certainly
never in an examination. For each issue or event you might experiment with using the three sub-headings, 'causes', 'what happened'
and 'consequences'. The headings and sub-headings used in the
chapter should help you to organise your notes. To complete your
notes on Liberal decline, you can look ahead to pages 92 and 115.

Answering structured and essay questions on Chapter 3

Sometimes material on the 1920s is included in questions on the
inter-war period as a whole (for examples, see chapters 4, 5 and 7).
However, several topics from the period 1922–9 are frequently the
subject of essay questions on their own.

A typical structured question on the first Labour Government is:

a) Why did many people fear a Labour administration in December 1923?
(*10 marks*)
b) What were Labour's achievement in office? (*15 marks*)
c) How far did Labour show that it was 'fit to govern' in 1924? (*25 marks*)

Parts a) and b) are straightforward, and you should be able to produce enough factual information to secure a good mark. Note, however, that there are more marks up for grabs in b), so that you are
expected to spend more time on what Labour actually did in office
than on the fears entertained beforehand. Section c) is altogether
more demanding: the emphasis here is on interpretation not fact,
and so there are as many marks available as for a) and b) combined.
Yet whereas c) on its own might be daunting, you have already done
much of the work in the earlier parts of the question. Clearly Labour
went a good way towards proving it was fit to govern if, in its nine
months in office, it calmed the somewhat wild and unrealistic fears
many had felt while the party was untested in office. (One way of
approaching a 'real' essay questions is, in fact, to imagine that it is the
final part of a stepped or structured question. What might the earlier
parts be? Such a technique will remove the mystique from essay questions by breaking them down into smaller, more manageable steps.)
Remember, for c), that we are concerned with people's judgements.
Labour only showed it was fit to govern if people thought it was. How
can we tell what people thought? The obvious answer is through the
1924 general election. Labour gained a million more votes, compared
with 1923, but many took the 'Red scare' seriously.

A standard essay question is:

I. Discuss the view that Baldwin's government of 1924–9 was 'a great reforming ministry'.

Attempt a first paragraph for this title. Clearly it will be necessary to try to define what is meant by 'a great reforming ministry'. There is no agreed definition of the phrase, so you will have to think very carefully about it. What *degree* of change must a government foster before it deserves to be called a reforming ministry? Does 'great' imply that changes were large-scale, effective and beneficial? You will also need to establish the important areas of reform in 1924–9. Should the return to the gold standard and the Trades Disputes Act be included? Remember that later in the essay you would have to justify what you include and show its relevance. Might you bring in the 1929 general election, and the Conservative strategy of 'safety first', to throw light on the achievements of this government? This could be mentioned, briefly, at the end of the paragraph, as you set up an argument. What are the possible overall arguments that might be used? Basically, you can either agree or disagree that it was a great reforming ministry. If you disagree, you can focus on the degree of continuity in these years. You can of course point out elements of change and continuity, but remember that you must answer the precise question set. Possibly you could both agree and disagree with the point of view put forward in the question by using two different definitions of 'great reforming ministry'. But this would be very difficult to do well and it is perhaps sensible to beware of being 'too clever by half'!

Source-based questions on Chapter 3

1. MacDonald writing to the King, 1924
Read the quotation from Ramsay MacDonald on page 54 and answer the following questions:

a) Why did MacDonald feel it necessary to state that Labour had proved its patriotism? (*2 marks*)
b) Why did MacDonald not stress Labour's differences from the other parties? (*3 marks*)
c) From your knowledge of the period, assess how accurate MacDonald's claims were. (*10 marks*)

2. The Liberal and Labour election manifestos of 1929
Read the extracts from *We can Conquer Unemployment* and *Labour and the Nation* on pages 63 and 64, and answer the following questions:

a) Was the Liberals' stress on the awful tragedy of unemployment more a reflection of existing general public concern or an attempt to create such a concern? Explain your answer. (*4 marks*)

b) Explain why the Liberals, while stressing the importance of state intervention, also pointed to the importance of 'individual enterprise'. (*3 marks*)

c) What do you understand by the phrases i) 'morality is in the nature of things' (page 65 line 4), and ii) 'men are, in very truth, members of one another' (page 65 line 5)? (*4 marks*)

d) What were 'the weapons' (page 65 line 6) used in the struggle for democracy and how might they be used to bring about socialism? (*4 marks*)

e) Why might the policies advocated by the two parties appeal to the electorate in the circumstances of 1929? (*10 marks*)

The Second Labour Government and the Crisis of 1931

4

POINTS TO CONSIDER

Labour was unlucky to win the election of 1929, since a formidable economic blizzard was soon to descend upon them. But might they, in office, have tackled Britain's problems with more skill and energy? As well as gaining a knowledge of what happened in 1929–31 you also have to make judgements. Were there viable alternative policies to Labour's economic orthodoxy? Was MacDonald right to form a coalition in 1931?

KEY DATES

1929 The Young Plan; (October) Wall Street Crash.
1930 London Naval Conference; Coal Mines Act; (May) the Mosley Memorandum; (Oct.) Mosley and MacDonald clashed at annual conference.
1931 (July) publication of the May Report, followed by a 'run on the pound'; (24 August), Labour cabinet split over cuts in unemployment benefits: MacDonald became prime minister of a National Government; (Sept.) MacDonald expelled from the Labour party; (21 Sept.) Britain abandoned gold standard; (27 October) general election: massive victory for the National Government.

1 The Second Labour Government

KEY ISSUE How did Labour grapple with the severe economic problems that beset Britain?

Several figures on the left urged Labour not to form a government after the 1929 election. They insisted that another minority administration would be powerless to introduce socialism and would therefore be pointless. But Labour's leaders paid little heed to such advice. They saw another opportunity to gain experience, to remove the last doubts about the party's fitness to govern and so to win over still more voters. MacDonald formed another cautious cabinet: Snowden was back at the Exchequer and this time there was no place for left-winger John Wheatley. The only innovation was the appointment of Britain's first woman cabinet minister, Margaret Bondfield, who became Minister of Labour. There was optimism in the air: unemployment totals had recently dipped and it seemed a good time to be in government. MacDonald told the House of Commons that he intended to continue in office for at least two years and that he would seek a broad consensus with the other parties. Privately he remarked that whereas in 1924 he had been 'a squatter, in constant danger of eviction', now he was 'a tenant with a lease'. He was more optimistic than for several years. He was also a little less lonely, having established friendships with several society ladies. He announced confidently that his government would tackle the two major problems of the day – unemployment and international friction.

a) Foreign Affairs

In foreign policy the second Labour government, like the first, achieved definite success. This time MacDonald (now 62) did not double as Foreign Secretary. He originally chose J.H. Thomas for this post but gave way when Arthur Henderson insisted that he would accept no other position. It was hard for MacDonald to resist the claims of such an experienced and widely respected colleague, even if he did not trust or like him. Yet MacDonald, who had always specialised in foreign affairs, was not prepared to stand aside totally. The result was a good deal of friction and rivalry with Henderson. But even so, Labour's achievement was substantial.

MacDonald was aware that naval rivalry had for some time been harming Anglo-American relations, and he himself took charge of this area of foreign policy. He visited Washington at the end of 1929 and held a naval conference in London the following year. Here agreement was reached on the relative tonnages of the British and American navies.

In European affairs, Henderson was the more influential, and he too enjoyed considerable success. Diplomatic relations were resumed with the Soviet Union, and a new reparations deal (the Young Plan) was agreed with Germany at the end of 1929. The following year it was arranged that the last allied troops occupying the Rhineland under the Treaty of Versailles would be removed five years ahead of schedule. Thus *détente* was being maintained in Europe.

b) Labour's Economic Policies

The real problems came in domestic affairs, although even here Labour did achieve some success. The rules were changed so that an applicant for unemployment benefit no longer had to prove that he was 'genuinely seeking work'. Instead, officials had to show that he had turned down a reasonable offer of work if they wished to stop his benefit. Also, the Coal Mines Act reduced the standard eight-hour shift by 30 minutes. But all was overshadowed by economic crisis. The fall in the number of unemployed workers in the summer of 1929 had been merely a blip. In October 1929 the stock market crashed in the United States (the Wall Street Crash), heralding not merely another periodic recession but the *Great Depression*, whose catastrophic effects were felt worldwide. Many commentators came to believe that capitalism itself might be collapsing and that the predictions of Karl Marx were finally being realised.

In Britain the full force of the economic downturn was felt. Between 1929 and 1931 the value of exports declined by nearly a half. Unemployment rose almost every month from November 1929 onwards: in July 1930 it topped the two million mark and in December 1930 it reached two and a half million. The cost of unemployment benefit, which had stood at £12 million in 1928, rocketed to £125 million in 1931. Whatever government had had the misfortune to be in office during this economic blizzard would have struggled to survive, let alone to solve the country's economic problems. In Germany and elsewhere the depression led to the overthrow of democracy. In Britain it led to unforeseen and unparalleled political developments.

The Prime Minister made J.H. Thomas head of a small ministerial team to tackle unemployment. The group also included the left-winger George Lansbury and a wealthy 33 year-old convert from the Conservative party, Sir Oswald Mosley. Thomas was soon able to claim that the government was spending £42 million on public works, but his approach was too unhurried and complacent for Mosley, who in May 1930 produced his own plan. Mosley wished to see protective tariffs to restrict imports, a greater use of credit to provide public works and promote expansion, more government direction of industry to promote rationalisation and efficiency, and increased pensions and allowances to boost domestic consumption and encourage earlier retirement. Borrowing ideas from Keynes, Lloyd George and the Conservative protectionists, he produced a positive package of proposals. He took the scheme to the cabinet, where it was hotly contested by both Thomas (whom he had not consulted) and the Chancellor. Snowden had always insisted on the necessity of balancing the budget and, in a time of declining government revenue, that meant cutting rather than increasing expenditure. Snowden's orthodoxy has seemed to some historians to be so rigid as to verge on bigotry. Symbolic of his devotion to convention was his insistence that the furniture in the Chancellor's office be restored to its traditional positions, after what he considered to be Churchill's unwarranted rearrangements!

The cabinet rejected Mosley's scheme in May 1930. Historians have speculated that if only he had been prepared to bide his time, he might have emerged eventually as the leader of his party. Instead, he resigned from the government and took his plans direct to the Parliamentary Labour Party and, in October, to Labour's annual conference. Again he was defeated, but only after a powerful speech:

1   They must go to parliament with an unemployment policy. If they were
     obstructed in parliament, then let them bring proposals before parlia-
     ment to reform it, so that they could get business through ... If their
     proposals were thrown out, they must go to the country and fight their
5   opponents on the question of unemployment and a revision of parlia-
     ment. At best, they would have their majority, at the worst they would
     go down fighting for the things they believed in. They would not die like
     an old woman in bed; they would die like a man in the field – a better
     fate, and, in politics, one with a more certain hope of resurrection.
10   He did not believe that the great national crisis they were living in
     was a menace to their Movement. It was their supreme opportunity ...
     Let them not shrink before a great opportunity; let them not shrink in
     fear before it; let them seize it and use it and give the country a lead.

Mosley was given one of the greatest ovations ever heard at a party
conference. But MacDonald's contribution to the debate was no less
skilful than Mosley's. The Prime Minister neatly deflected criticisms
of the government for the country's economic ills:

1   So, my friends, we are not on trial; it is the system under which we live.
     It has broken down, not only in this little island; it has broken down in
     Europe, in Asia, in America; it has broken down everywhere as it was
     bound to break down ... I appeal to you, my friends today, with all that
5   is going on outside – I appeal to you to go back on to your socialist faith.
     Do not mix that up with pettifogging patching – either of a Poor Law
     kind or of Relief Work kind. Construction, ideas, architecture, building
     line upon line, stone upon stone, storey upon storey; it will not be your
     happiness, it will certainly not be mine, to see that fabric finished ... But
10   I think it will be your happiness, as it is mine, to go on convinced that
     the great foundations are being laid ... and that ... the temple will rise
     and rise until at last it is complete, and the genius of humanity will find
     within it an appropriate resting place.

Mosley was defeated by party loyalty – so that political stability ruled
out economic radicalism – and by the emotional appeal of socialism
as a visionary faith.

It has been rightly said, by Robert Skidelsky, that MacDonald's
socialism was utopian, explaining the past and promising the future
but with nothing positive to offer the present. MacDonald had no
'theory of the transition', no method of transforming capitalism into
socialism. He simply hoped that one day socialist reforms could be
paid for out of a successful capitalism. Hence he had little idea of how
to cope with the failing economy. (See Low's cartoon, 'Cart before
the Horse' on page 75.)

The rejection of his proposals led Mosley to enter the political
wilderness, founding a new political party in 1931 and soon despair-
ing of democracy altogether. The main result of his campaign was
that MacDonald himself took charge of unemployment policy,
although he had never specialised in economic affairs and was in

'The Cart before the Horse', by David Low.

many ways out of his depth. He set up commissions and committees to investigate aspects of Britain's economic woes, but more to gain a breathing-space than to hear their verdicts. While they were investigating, the government would survive and possibly the depression might end by itself. However, in 1931 things got even worse.

c) The Crisis Deepens

There was no easy solution for Labour to turn to. MacDonald appointed a 15-man economic advisory council – a 'think tank' – including Keynes, to provide alternatives to Treasury thinking, but there were certainly no successful precedents for the government to follow. Keynes told MacDonald that he had to choose between 'enterprise' and 'thrift'. He himself was all in favour of the former, and he called for large-scale public works or deficit financing ('reflation'), but such ideas were closely associated with Lloyd George and Oswald Mosley. The fact that Labour had rejected Mosley's package in 1930 made it politically difficult to accept similar measures in 1931, even though the economic climate was by then so much worse. MacDonald's bid for 'respectability' and moderate policies also made it very hard for him to take risks by adopting untried, radical approaches. Expenditure on public works rose from £70 million in February to £140 million in September 1930. The weight of orthodox advice was in favour of cuts in government spending ('deflation') and of waiting for better times. This was Snowden's preferred policy. But retrenchment would mean cuts in socially valuable services – perhaps even in unemployment benefit – which the bulk of the Labour cabinet was most unwilling to accept. The alternative was simply drift, and this was the policy (if that term be applicable) to which Labour clung: the budget was left unbalanced (i.e. government expenditure was allowed to exceed government revenue) for as long as possible.

Britain's financial problems stemmed in part from the return to the gold standard in 1925. This had several disadvantages. The high exchange value of sterling (at $4.86) meant that British exports were uncompetitive; and in addition Britain had to maintain the exchange rate by keeping interest rates high (in order to encourage overseas investors to keep their money in Britain). The Bank of England also had to use its gold reserves to buy the pounds of those investors who wished to sell their holdings. International confidence was essential for Britain to maintain the gold standard; otherwise overseas holders of sterling would rush to sell pounds for gold or other currencies. However, it was clear that foreign confidence would evaporate if the budget were left unbalanced for long. Hence Snowden put pressure on his cabinet colleagues for cuts. MacDonald came to believe that protective tariffs were needed: the revenue so raised might enable the budget to be balanced, thus reducing the need for retrenchment. But the Prime Minister, who sometimes wished that Snowden would bow out of active politics and accept a seat in the Lords, was not certain enough of economic theory to challenge his free-trading Chancellor.

MacDonald found his position entirely uncongenial. In the middle of 1930, after a poor speech, he noted in his diary: 'said what I did not want to say and did not say what I wanted'. He was feeling worn out 'and my head would not work'. Later in the year he felt 'dead and wonder more and more if it is possible to go on. Flesh and nerves can hardly stand it'. He was becoming more isolated and jumpy and began to fear that Henderson was after his job. Lloyd George described him at this time as 'as near a broken man as I have seen in a big job'. The following year things got worse and in the summer of 1931 crisis erupted. MacDonald's commissions did what they had not been set up to do – they concluded their investigations.

A Royal Commission on unemployment insurance reported, calling for reductions of up to 30 per cent in unemployment benefit. The following month, in July, the all-party May Commission recommended a 20 per cent cut. Keynes called the May Report 'the most foolish document I ever had the misfortune to read'. But the Commissioners' advice, following the collapse of banks in Europe (and the loss of British investments) and coinciding with a severe balance of payments crisis, seemed to make it essential for the government to take decisive action. Snowden insisted that retrenchment should replace drift. A 'run on the pound' occurred, stimulated partly by the gloom of the May report: foreign investors, fearing that Britain faced bankruptcy, began to withdraw funds in alarming quantities. By the end of July 1931 almost a quarter of the Bank of England's gold reserves had been used up. Snowden was convinced of the need to borrow money from international bankers to maintain the gold standard. But a condition of the loan, he insisted, was budget cuts. Would a Labour cabinet take the unpopular action of cutting unemployment benefit? In the summer of 1931 ministers were recalled from their holidays for key cabinet meetings. August 1931 was to be a decisive month in modern British politics.

2 The Fall of Labour

KEY ISSUE How and why did Labour go out of office?

On 19 August MacDonald's cabinet sat from 11 in the morning until 10.30 at night, wrangling about the extent of cuts in government expenditure. Over the next few days ministers were in an almost constant debate, the key issue being whether unemployment benefit should be cut.

To Snowden it was clear that there was no other practicable choice. Unless there was at least a 10 per cent cut in the standard rates of benefit then the budget could not be balanced, and if the budget was not balanced then bankers in New York and Paris would be unwilling to lend Britain the money it needed. The group in the cabinet which supported Snowden pointed out that a 10 per cent reduction would merely restore the levels paid before the increases Labour had instituted back in 1924, and since then prices had fallen considerably. The economist Maynard Keynes proposed an alternative strategy. He urged that Britain should suspend the gold standard. The pound would then sink in value, British exports would be more competitive and so Britain's balance of payments deficit would ease. In addition, if sterling were not tied to gold, the Bank of England would not have to deplete its gold reserves to maintain the inflated value of the pound. Yet his was a (sophisticated) voice in the wilderness: of the leading figures in Labour's ranks, only the trade unionist leader Ernest Bevin supported him. The huge majority of those who opposed cuts in the dole did so not because of financial theory but as a gut reaction: Labour's primary purpose was to secure a better deal for the underprivileged, not to impose sacrifices on those least able to bear them. Henderson and others believed that the unemployed were already the victims of capitalism and that it would be unacceptable for a Labour government to victimise them further. A delegation to the cabinet from the Trades Union Congress lent its considerable weight to this resistance to cuts.

MacDonald brushed aside the unorthodox recommendations of Keynes and decided to support his Chancellor. The Labour government, he believed, had to act responsibly: it was the government of the whole country and not the mouthpiece of the unions or the working class. It had to take whatever decisions were in the national interest, even at the risk of unpopularity with a majority of its own supporters. The Prime Minister did his utmost to secure cabinet support for reduced expenditure, and the cabinet did agree unanimously to cutbacks totalling £56 million. However, this figure did not include a 10 per cent cut in unemployment benefit. MacDonald and Snowden were not satisfied: they insisted on reductions of £78 million, including the 10 per cent cut.

According to the cabinet records, MacDonald told his colleagues that:

1   a scheme which inflicted reductions and burdens in almost every other direction, but made no appreciable cut in Unemployment Insurance benefit, would alienate much support and lose the party their moral prestige which was one of their greatest assets. In conclusion, the prime
5   minister said that it must be admitted that the proposals as a whole represented the negation of everything the Labour party stood for, and yet he was absolutely satisfied that it was necessary, in the national interest, to implement them if the country was to be secured.

Philip Snowden, the Chancellor, also insisted that there was no real alternative to the cuts. As far as he was concerned:

> 1 He had no doubt whatever that, if he was compelled to choose
> between retaining the Labour Movement in its present form and reduc-
> ing the standard of living of the workmen by 50 per cent which would
> be the effect of departing from the Gold Standard he knew where his
> 5 duty would lie.

Yet one group of ministers remained immovable. Henderson – who
knew even less of finance and economics than MacDonald – insisted
that cuts in unemployment benefit, whatever the circumstances,
would be regarded as a betrayal of trust by Labour voters. The unemployed were 'their people'. Instead he called for the government to
resign: if reductions in the standard of living of the unemployed were
necessary, other parties – and not Labour – should impose them.
Beatrice Webb noted in her diary that:

> 1 It is the financiers, British and American, who will settle the personnel
> and policy of the British Government ... The Dictatorship of the
> Capitalist with a vengeance! Henderson blames the PM for spending so
> much time in negotiation: he thinks it would have been far better to
> 5 have settled really what the Labour Cabinet would be prepared to do
> in economies and resign if it were rejected by the Opposition ... The
> plain truth is that the Labour Prime Minister, Chancellor of the
> Exchequer, together with the ineffable Jimmy [Thomas] are converted
> to the capitalist creed and would be quite contented to carry it out if
> 10 the party would agree to let them!

MacDonald and Henderson were each convinced that the other was
betraying important ideals. The two most senior figures in the Labour
party had never liked each other, but now the breach between them
was complete. When a final vote was taken, the cabinet split 11–9 in
favour of the £78 million package of cuts. No government divided in
this way could survive. MacDonald decided to resign as prime minister; and if Labour in opposition opposed cuts, he would resign as
party leader as well.

a) How Successful was the Second Labour Government?

The second Labour government was effectively over. An excellent,
brief epitaph was provided by a junior minister, Hugh Dalton: 'The
second Labour Government's record abroad is a moderate success
story, not lacking courage and skill. Its record at home is a hard-luck
story, with failure almost unredeemed by either courage or skill.'
Labour had done well abroad and at home they did have the bad luck
to be in office, as a minority government, at a time of unparalleled
economic depression. The charge against Labour is not that they
failed – for perhaps they had no chance of success – but that they
made no real attempt to solve Britain's economic ills. Their rhetoric
was radical whilst their actions were puny. Positive proposals might
well have failed to get through the Commons, though Lloyd George

always promised to support progressive measures and the Tories would certainly have supported protection or retrenchment. But Labour ministers did little more than hope for the best and mark time, and in the end they split when they could no longer avoid positive proposals. Their 'socialism' was impractical: they did not know whether to rejoice that their predictions about the evils and instability of capitalism had been borne out or to weep at their misfortune of being in office.

3 The Formation of the National Government

> **KEY ISSUE** Was there a conspiracy to remove Labour from office?

The other area of controversy concerning the Labour government centres on the way it went out of office. In 1924, with the Zinoviev letter, Labour had believed itself the victim of an underhand capitalist plot. Now in 1931 it came to see itself once more as a martyr, intrigued out of office by a conspiracy of international bankers and by the ambitions of Ramsay MacDonald. MacDonald left the cabinet on 24 August to offer his resignation to the king. He returned from the Palace as Prime Minister of a coalition government. Labour's leader was said to have betrayed his party and the working class: he had become the 'Lucifer of the Left'.

The establishment of an all-party coalition in August 1931 is the most controversial political event in Britain in the twentieth century, and the one most surrounded with myths. Many prejudiced accounts have been written of the confused period from 20 to 24 August. MacDonald has been accused of betraying the Labour party and indeed of planning in advance for months, if not years, to do so. He is said to have been corrupted by the 'establishment' and to have fallen victim to the 'aristocratic embrace'. MacDonald, rubbing his hands gleefully, was quoted, shortly after the formation of the national government, as insisting that 'tomorrow every Duchess in London will be wanting to kiss me!' At the same time, the downfall of the Labour government was thought to have been engineered by international bankers, anxious to get rid of a socialist government. The crisis was the result of a 'bankers' ramp'.

The reality was much less sensational. Certainly there had been no bankers' conspiracy. Admittedly financiers in New York and Paris had insisted on a balanced budget as a precondition for a loan, but this was normal commercial procedure. They simply wished to protect their investment, not to eject the Labour government. In truth, over the previous years Labour had shown itself no enemy of capitalism. The 'bankers' ramp' theory greatly exaggerates the threat that Labour's 'socialism' posed to the financial establishment.

Nor was MacDonald the villain depicted by many aggrieved left-wingers. There is no evidence that he had planned his actions long in advance. He was no mastermind able to control events. On the contrary, he was all but overwhelmed by circumstances. He had originally intended to resign when his cabinet could not agree on expenditure cuts, but instead he was persuaded by others to remain as prime minister of a 'national government'.

King George V had several times suggested to MacDonald that a coalition was advisable. Coalitions in peacetime were rare, but the results of the 1929 election had necessitated some form of inter-party cooperation and the problems of 1931, with almost 3 million unemployed, seemed comparable in their magnitude to those of a war. Now the King took the initiative in persuading MacDonald to stay on. It was his duty to do so: resignation would be a form of desertion. According to Vernon Bogdanor, George V 'was not merely the facilitator ... but the instigator' of the national government. As such, he may well have exceeded his constitutional powers.

Opposition politicians added their voices to the chorus. MacDonald had met the Conservative and Liberal leaders frequently over the previous months. He had not been hatching his long-desired coalition plot but had, quite properly in view of his government's lack of a majority, been sounding out their reaction to various lines of policy and warning them that they might have to form a government themselves. Lloyd George was at this time in hospital, but the acting leader of the Liberals, Herbert Samuel, pressed on MacDonald the importance of a coalition. Probably the Liberals did not want the expense of another election, and Samuel believed that a coalition was perhaps their only route back into government.

Neville Chamberlain, one of the leading Conservatives, also saw the advantages of an all-party government. A doer not a speech-maker, he disliked being in opposition. Moreover he believed that the expenditure cuts were vital for the nation's survival. Chamberlain insisted that a coalition led by MacDonald would carry much greater weight abroad than a purely Conservative government. More selfishly, he saw that a coalition would split Labour and so benefit the Tories. As for Baldwin, he had no enthusiasm for a coalition after the example of 1918–22 and believed that the most obvious course was for Labour to resign, for a Tory government to make the cuts, and then for a general election to be held. However, at least he was not being asked to work alongside Lloyd George, whom he hated so much. Cajoled by the King and Chamberlain, he relented. The Conservative leader urged MacDonald to stay on and agreed to serve under him.

MacDonald acquiesced in this pressure and arranged that Snowden and J.H. Thomas would join him. He had not deliberately betrayed the Labour party; he simply felt that the party – or rather the nine cabinet ministers who refused to accept cuts in unemployment benefit – were betraying the nation. Given his acceptance of the need for retrenchment, he made a well-reasoned decision. His actions also stemmed from his past – from his decision to make Labour a national, rather than a trade union or class party; from his specialisation in foreign rather than economic issues; and from his aloof and detached personality which left a gulf between himself and the bulk of his colleagues and supporters. He had always been less a leader, who had taken Labour supporters with him, than Labour's star performer.

Overall MacDonald's motives in forming the National Government were probably mixed. A newspaper story on the setting up of the new government bore the headline 'Thank God for Him' (i.e. MacDonald). An element of vanity almost certainly played its part in his decision to continue in office. As Taylor has noted, 'few repudiate the title of saviour when it is offered to them'. But there is also truth in the same historian's judgement that, 'his primary motive was patriotism'. He genuinely believed that he was acting in the national interest. Perhaps he hoped that he could return to Labour when the coalition was no longer required. Certainly, he announced that the National Government was to be temporary. It was to deal with the national emergency, to balance the budget by cuts in expenditure and to save the pound. After that there was to be a return to normal party politics. But the Labour party lost little time in choosing Arthur Henderson as its leader, and at the end of September MacDonald was formally expelled. Now he had no party to which he could return. Labour was in fact relieved to have got rid of him. Henderson seemed a more trustworthy and loyal man and, after a gruelling 20 months, most Labour MPs welcomed a spell in opposition. They were content to let the National Government make expenditure cuts: Labour's ex-ministers now unanimously opposed the retrenchment which, in office, most of them had been prepared to accept.

4 The National Government in Action

> **KEY ISSUE** What impact did the new government have on the financial crisis?

The national government was formed on 24 August 1931 as a temporary expedient. It was called into existence in an extreme financial emergency to balance the budget and to 'save the pound'. It quickly did the former, but failed to achieve the latter. Snowden, who continued as Chancellor, made economies of £70 million in government expenditure, including a 10 per cent cut in unemployment benefit. He also increased taxation, lifting the standard rate of income tax from 22.5 per cent to 25 per cent. These measures balanced the budget and allowed the government to negotiate a loan from abroad. But, nevertheless, Britain was soon forced off the gold standard.

Snowden's economies cut not only unemployment benefit but also the salaries of government employees, and on 15 September British sailors in the fleet at Invergordon (on the Scottish coast), some of whose pay had been reduced by more than 10 per cent, protested by refusing to obey orders. News of the 'Invergordon mutiny' produced a flight from sterling. Foreign holders of pounds moved quickly to cash in their investments, as there was little point holding on to a currency which almost everyone realised was over-valued. Britain's gold reserves were soon dangerously depleted. Montagu Norman, the Governor of the Bank of England, with extreme reluctance, recommended that the gold standard should be abandoned. Many people expected dire consequences to follow, including rapid inflation, and the pound fell from $4.86 to around $3.40. But it was soon realised that this devaluation of sterling was largely beneficial as it resulted in a more realistic exchange rate. The gold standard had been a 'sacred cow' which had needlessly complicated Britain's economic problems.

5 The General Election of 1931

KEY ISSUE Why was the general election such a landslide?

The National Government had now ceased to have much reason to exist. Some thought that normal party politics would be resumed. However, MacDonald was pressured by the Conservatives to hold a general election and to perpetuate the all-party coalition. Disowned by Labour and lacking a party of his own, he found it impossible to resist these demands and a general election was held on 27 October 1931. Having carried out its commitment to make budget cuts, the government had few precise policies to offer. Many Conservatives wanted to introduce protective tariffs, but such an issue would lead to disagreements with the Liberal free-traders and with Snowden. Hence the government simply asked for a vote of confidence – a 'doctor's mandate' – and bent its energies to criticising the Labour opposition. Fought in an atmosphere described as 'jingoistic panic', the election was a bruising contest. Snowden turned on his former Labour colleagues and, in a radio broadcast, stigmatised their programme as 'Bolshevism run mad'. He also resurrected an old bogey, insisting that, if Labour won, people's post office savings would be in danger. Many electors were genuinely scared.

Party	General Election, 27 October 1931		
	No. of votes	Percentage of total votes	Seats
Conservative	11,978,745	55.24	73
National Labour	341,370	1.6	13
National Liberal	2,212,404	10.2	68
National Government	14,532,519	67	554
Independent Liberal	106,106	0.5	4
Labour	6,649,630	30.6	52

It was the greatest electoral landslide of the century. In 1918 the coalition had won less than half the total vote. Now the national government took a massive 67 per cent of the vote and a staggering 90 per cent of seats.

The Liberals, whose percentage of the total vote had fallen from over 23 per cent to under 11 per cent, had again been split. The majority supported the coalition, while Lloyd George repudiated it, calling the election 'a partisan intrigue under the guise of a patriotic appeal'. (He was also scathing on Samuel, joking that when the doctor circumcised him as a baby, he threw away the wrong bit.) But he and his followers could muster only four seats. Oswald Mosley's 'New Party' fared even worse, all 24 of its candidates being defeated. But the main victims were Labour. Their total of seats sank from 288 to a mere 52. Even Henderson was defeated, and the election saw some spectacular Labour reverses. In Gateshead, where at the previous election Labour had enjoyed a majority of nearly 17,000, they now suffered a defeat by 13,000 votes. The British parliamentary system magnified the national swing. The popular vote for Labour still stood at over 30 per cent, and the party polled more votes than in any previous election except 1929. But this was small comfort for a party that had been reduced to a rump of an opposition.

Labour supporters had been quite pleased to be free of MacDonald back in August; now they turned with venom on their former leader as the traitor who had caused their troubles:

> We'll hang Ramsay Mac on a sour apple tree,
> We'll hang Snowden and Thomas to keep him company;
> For that's the place where traitors ought to be.

MacDonald had become a convenient scapegoat, so that Labour's own responsibility for the failures of 1929–31 could be forgotten. He was a saviour to some, and a villain to others. Probably he deserves neither description.

Summary Diagram
The second Labour Government and the crisis of 1931

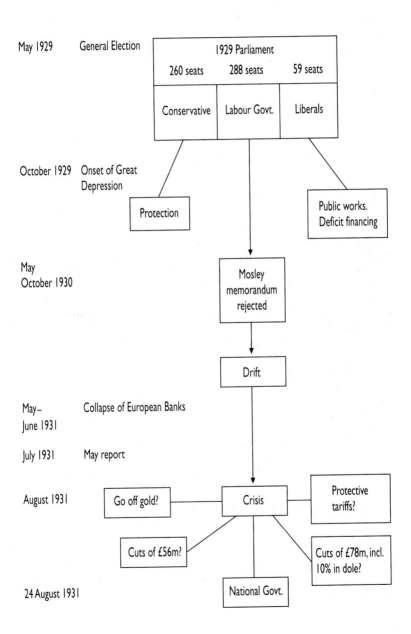

May 1929	General Election
October 1929	Onset of Great Depression
May October 1930	
May– June 1931	Collapse of European Banks
July 1931	May report
August 1931	
24 August 1931	

1929 Parliament

260 seats — 288 seats — 59 seats

Conservative | Labour Govt. | Liberals

Protection

Public works. Deficit financing

Mosley memorandum rejected

Drift

Go off gold?

Crisis

Protective tariffs?

Cuts of £56m?

Cuts of £78m, incl. 10% in dole?

National Govt.

Working on Chapter 4

You need to make detailed notes on this chapter. The simplest way in which to do this would be to follow the pattern of headings used in the text and to summarise the facts and arguments presented as briefly as possible. But do engage with the key issues – how well or badly Labour performed, whether they should have pursued other policies, and why a National Government was formed.

Answering essay questions on Chapter 4

Most questions on the years 1929–31 combine the work of the second Labour government with the formation of the National Government. Therefore you need to display a knowledge of the economic and political problems the depression brought about and of the crisis of July and August 1931. Consider the following question:

1. Do you agree that Labour was 'betrayed' by Ramsay MacDonald in 1931?

You might break down the essay into several smaller issues, as in a structured question:

a) The background (minority position, economic problems) which made problems for MacDonald inevitable.
b) Labour's policies and the issue of whether other viable policies existed.
c) MacDonald's background; his personal responsibility for economic strategy.
d) The cabinet clashes of August 1931. Why did MacDonald insist on cuts? Was he betraying the unemployed, or did he think he was serving the interests of the nation as a whole? Was Henderson the true representative of 'socialism'?
e) Formation of the National Government. Was MacDonald in charge of events? Was he primarily concerned with his own future, that of the Labour party, or the nation as a whole?

Sometimes questions combine the first and second Labour governments. Here are several examples:

2. Consider the view that Labour's failure in office between the wars was due to the fact that its leaders were 'insufficiently socialist'.
3. 'Fruitful but unhappy experiences of government.' How far do you agree with this view of MacDonald's two Labour governments?
4. 'The two interwar Labour governments were as successful as circumstances permitted.' Examine this view of the Labour administrations of 1924 and 1929–31.

Construct first paragraphs for these titles. Begin by defining their key terms. Clearly you must make up your own mind about the most important causes of Labour's failures, and especially about whether circumstances made failure inevitable. There is scope for a wide variety of interpretations, but the important thing is to be clear in your thinking and to have evidence to back up your argument.

Source-based Questions on Chapter 4

1. Mosley and MacDonald at the 1931 Labour Party Conference

Read the extracts from the speeches made by Sir Oswald Mosley and Ramsay MacDonald at Labour's annual conference in October 1931, given on page 74, and answer the following questions:

a) What constitutional reforms might Mosley have been hinting at? (*4 marks*)

b) Explain in detail the likely reasons why Mosley's speech received such a great ovation. (*5 marks*)

c) Why did MacDonald say that the system was 'bound to break down'? (*3 marks*)

d) Explain what MacDonald meant by 'pettifogging patching'. Why was he hostile to it? (*5 marks*)

e) In what ways do the two speeches reveal the nature of Labour's socialism around 1930? (*8 marks*)

2. Low's cartoon, 'Cart before the Horse'

Study Low's cartoon on page 75 and answer the following questions:

a) MacDonald is the man on the cart pointing the way forward. What statement about him has Low made by the way he has chosen to portray him? (*4 marks*)

b) Who are the passengers? What sort of people are represented by 'Etc, Etc'? (*5 marks*)

c) What was Low's opinion of the government's unemployment policy? How far was this judgement justified? (*7 marks*)

d) Explain the meaning of the cartoon's caption. (*4 marks*)

3. MacDonald, Snowden and Beatrice Webb on the 1931 crisis

Read the extracts given on pages 78–9, and answer the following questions:

a) What did MacDonald mean by 'moral prestige' (page 78 line 4)? With which groups would it be lost? (*4 marks*)

b) In what sense did the proposals represent the 'negation of everything the Labour Party stood for' (page 78 line 6)? (*2 marks*)

c) For what reasons did Snowden believe that the departure from the gold

standard would reduce the standard of living of workers by 50 per cent?
(*4 marks*)
d) What strategy is Henderson reported as supporting? How does this differ from the policy of MacDonald and his supporters? (*5 marks*)
e) Assess the reliability of the extracts as evidence of the views and opinions of MacDonald, Snowden and Henderson at the time. (*5 marks*)
f) How completely do the three statements reveal the diversity of opinion that existed on financial policy within Britain at this time? (*10 marks*)

5 The National Government, 1931–9

POINTS TO CONSIDER

A wide variety of issues is dealt with in this chapter. Try to gain a good knowledge of them all but also to judge which issues were of most significance. How important, for instance, was the Abdication Crisis compared with policy towards India? Also, try to see if there are connections between the policies pursued in different areas. Did the government display the same attitudes of mind in its approach to unemployment and to Hitler's aggression?

KEY DATES

1931 (Sept.) Japan invaded Manchuria.
1932 (Feb.) Import Duties Bill: 'agreement to differ' with free-traders; (June) Lausanne Conference, effectively ending reparations; (July–August) Ottawa Conference; (Sept.) Liberal free-traders and Snowden resigned.
1933 Hitler came to power in Germany.
1934 Unemployment Act, creating the Unemployment Assistant Board.
1935 Special Areas Act; Government of India Act; (April) Stresa Front; (June) Baldwin replaced MacDonald as PM; (14 Nov.) general election victory for National Government (Conservatives); (Dec.)Hoare-Laval Plan, resignation of Hoare.
1936 (Jan.) Death of George V; (March) Hitler remilitarised the Rhineland; (Dec.) Abdication Crisis, George VI succeeding Edward VIII.
1937 Factory Act; (28 May) Neville Chamberlain succeeded Baldwin.
1938 Coal Mines Act, nationalising mining royalties; (Feb.) Eden resigned as Foreign Secretary; (March) Hitler annexed Austria; (Sept.) Munich conference: Sudetenland ceded to Germany.
1939 British Overseas Airways Corporation established; (March) Hitler invaded rest of Czechoslovakia; (Sept) start of Second World War.

1 The Political Scene, 1931–5

KEY ISSUE Where did real power lie in the National Government?

The national government won such an overwhelming victory in the general election of 1931 that there was no real opposition in parliament. Yet this situation was not expected to last for long. The Lloyd George coalition had broken up in the end, and this one was

expected to be no different. It could plausibly be argued that a
national emergency existed in October 1931, justifying the continuation of the coalition, but the government's days seemed numbered.
It would surely either solve the crisis and be redundant, or it would
fail and so fall from office. In fact a coalition which, at its beginning,
had been designed to be one of the shortest in modern history turned
out to be the longest. It ran almost its full term and then fought the
1935 election as a united government. Yet the national government
did not survive unchanged until 1935. It became more and more obvious that the Conservatives were overwhelmingly dominant. In August
1931 the cabinet had comprised four Labour men, four Tories and
two Liberals. After the election in October, there were 11 Tories and
nine others in a larger cabinet, and by 1935 there were 15 Tories
and seven others.

a) National Labour

The Prime Minister of the national government, Ramsay MacDonald,
was, like Lloyd George before him, a 'prime minister without a party'.
In other ways he certainly did not resemble LG. In 1918–22 the
Conservatives had complained of the Prime Minister's dominance;
there were no such complaints of MacDonald. He had been unable to
resist Tory calls for an election in October 1931, and the election
results made him even more aware of Conservative predominance,
symbolised by Snowden's 'elevation' to the House of Lords and his
replacement by Neville Chamberlain as Chancellor of the Exchequer.

MacDonald was the prisoner of the Tories but he was no mere figurehead, at least not at first. As in the two Labour governments, he
had an important and constructive impact on foreign affairs. It was
partly due to his influence that at the Lausanne conference in June
1932 an effective end was made to reparation payments, to be followed shortly by war-debts. Yet there were clear signs that his health
and faculties were deteriorating. Years of excessive work were taking
their toll, particularly of his eyesight. In January 1932 he underwent
an operation for glaucoma of the left eye, and a few months later his
right eye needed similar treatment. By the end of the year, as his
insomnia became worse than ever, he described himself as suffering
from 'a complete breakdown, from top to toe, inside and out'. His
speeches, always emotional and imprecise, became more long-winded
and vague than ever.

By 1935 'Ramsay Mac' was widely referred to as 'Ramshackle Mac'.
Baldwin commented that 'it was tragic to see him in his closing days
as prime minister, losing the thread of his speech and turning to ask
a colleague why people were laughing – detested by his old friends,
despised by Conservatives.' In June 1935 he was eased out of the premiership and was succeeded by Baldwin – not, as in his confusion he
supposed, by Chamberlain. Even then he did not retire, staying on in

the cabinet as Lord President of the Council. At the end of the year he addressed the small 'National Labour' group in the Commons, trying to rally his supporters and identify the common principles that united them. One of those present described the occasion:

1 'We shall', said Ramsay, 'be neither red, white nor blue. We stand for Labour within the Baldwin organisation. We shall further the aims of the organisation but we shall remain OURSELVES.' Having said that, he struck the arm of his chair with a clenched fist and gazed upwards to
5 where, above the mantelpiece, God was most likely to be found. 'OUR-SELVES' he repeated fervently, like a Covenanter dedicating his sword and buckler. We did not like to look at each other so awkward were our feelings ... and in acute embarrassment we broke up.

By this time, the National Labour MPs were a meaningless political rump, an irrelevancy whose sole purpose seemed to be to disguise Conservative domination and to give some credibility to the notion of a 'national' government. J.H. Thomas resigned in 1936, after leaking budget secrets for financial gain. MacDonald resigned from the government in 1937, the year of his death.

b) The Achievements of Ramsay MacDonald

MacDonald's last years were inglorious, and he would have done better to retire earlier. But neither the decline of his powers nor the exaggerated charges of 'traitor' levelled at him from the left since 1931 should detract from a proper historical assessment of his achievements.

First, it should be said that he had done much to bring the Labour party into parliament and into office. His moderate policies helped to attract uncommitted voters. He, more than any other individual, made Labour into the main challenger to the Conservatives. For several decades he was a dominant and popular political personality, easily outshining more pedestrian and rigid colleagues like Henderson and Snowden. Admittedly his socialism was emotional and perhaps utopian, so that he had far more ideals than practical ideas, but this was a characteristic failing of many left-wing thinkers of the time. His role in the formation of the national government will long remain controversial, but few historians today believe that he deliberately betrayed his party. He may have been misguided, but he acted with the best intentions. He consciously put country before party and courageously refused to run away from a crisis. He was expelled from the Labour party but, even so, the party could not undo his work or his influence, and the progressive Labour government of 1945–51 has been called his monument. He was also, as his major biographer, David Marquand, has argued, a decent and like-able man, vain and suspicious but not snobbish or mean-spirited, who had a genuine faith in the possibility of co-operation between nations.

c) The Liberals in the National Govenment

The unity achieved by the Liberal party in the late-1920s proved to be paper thin. The 1931 crisis detached Lloyd George from the bulk of Liberal MPs, and after the 1931 election two very distinct developed among those Liberals who supported the government. Sir John Simon emerged as leader of 35 Liberal National MPs (or 'Simonites'): these were separate from the Conservatives but very hard to distinguish from them. They even abandoned their former commitment to free trade. Simon was rewarded by high office. During the 1930s he was sucessively Foreign Secretary, Home Secretary and Chancellor of the Exchequer.

The remaining 33 Liberal MPs, led by the official party leader Sir Herbert Samuel, supported the government but did so far more reservedly. In particular, the 'Samuelites' retained their commitment to free trade. In February 1932, when a measure of protection was introduced, these Liberals only remained in the government when the doctrine of collective cabinet responsibility (the notion that all cabinet ministers were collectively responsible for policy and so had to support cabinet decisions) was temporarily suspended. Baldwin announced that the cabinet was unanimous in its collective decision to suspend collective responsibility. But this unique – and perhaps unconstitutional – suspension of political tradition did not last long. Later in the year, with the adoption of a more permanent measure of protection, the Liberal free-traders (along with Philip Snowden) resigned from the government. At first the Liberals sat on the government back benches, and so could not unite with Lloyd George's few followers. But a year later they 'crossed the floor' and joined the opposition. MacDonald had urged them not to go, insisting correctly that his own position would become 'more and more degraded … I should be regarded as a limpet in office'. But they had taken no notice, and the split between the Simonites and Samuelites was complete. The coalition was more clearly dominated by the Conservatives than ever before.

d) Stanley Baldwin

The Conservatives were overwhelmingly dominant in the House of Commons after 1931. Their leader, Stanley Baldwin, although not prime minister until 1935, was the single most influential figure in the government, the power behind the throne. Thus there had been an amazing transformation in Baldwin's political position.

Few had expected him to survive long as Conservative leader after the election of 1929. The whole Conservative campaign had been so built around him that defeat was a severe and personal blow. Quite simply, he no longer seemed an electoral asset. Nor was he an impressive leader of an opposition party: he was too much the fair and reasonable conciliator and not enough the destructive critic. His enemies saw their opportunity. In particular, the newspaper proprietor Lord Beaverbrook decided that there had to be new leadership, together with new policies. 'Safety First' had been too uninspiring and something more positive was needed. Beaverbrook decided that that something was protection, or rather a variation of protection, 'empire free trade'. His idea was that the British empire, which comprised one-quarter of the world's land surface, should become a free trading area, protected by high tariff barriers from the rest of the world. Beaverbrook sponsored 'united empire' candidates, one of whom defeated the official Conservative candidate in a by-election in October 1930. Baldwin agreed to resign, but then had a change of heart and won public support by denouncing the press barons. He insisted that they wanted 'power without responsibility – the prerogative of the harlot throughout the ages' (words be borrowed from his cousin Rudyard Kipling). Baldwin's position was temporarily secure, but few expected that he could carry on as party leader for much longer. The formation of the national government, and the ending of normal party politics, was thus greatly to his advantage.

Baldwin occupied what was traditionally the Chancellor's house, 11 Downing Street, which had an interconnecting door with Number 10. He was able to work closely with MacDonald, and usually to dominate the Prime Minister. After all, while MacDonald led a party of 13 MPs, Baldwin was leader of 473. But this is not to say that from 1931 to 1935 the National Government was merely a Tory facade, as many historians have assumed. Baldwin told the 1932 Conservative party conference that 'our aims must be national and not party; our ideals must be national and not party' – and he meant what he said.

Baldwin was always a moderate and had wanted to pursue progressive and 'national', as opposed to class, policies. It was for this reason that he was so disliked by the diehard wing of his party, members of which complained that his ideas were 'half-way to socialism'. As prime minister of a Conservative government, Baldwin had not been able to put into practice his brand of moderate Conservatism. The Trade Disputes Act of 1927 (see page 59) had shown this. But now the national government provided ideal conditions for a man of his political complexion. Only moderate Conservative policies could hope to win the support of the Labour and Liberal men in the coalition, support that was needed to sustain the 'national' ethos which had been so important at the 1931 election. Too many Conservatives had won their seats under the national banner for them to underestimate its importance for the electorate. There were even plans to bring about 'fusion': to join the wings of the government into a new 'national' party.

Baldwin had finally found a way to silence his critics. His prestige in the government and in the country as a whole had reached new heights. He also enjoyed politics much more than before. A civil servant wrote of him in 1933: 'This being second and not first suits him perfectly and frees him from final decisions and from worry.' He had found the position that best matched his temperament and his philosophy. Hence he was in no hurry to replace MacDonald as prime minister and, perhaps out of a misguided sense of loyalty, allowed the Labour premier to stay even when his physical and mental powers had deteriorated. Not that Baldwin was in peak physical condition himself. In November 1932 an observer noted that he was going deaf: 'He often does not hear me despite my loud voice and clear speech.' Baldwin was not physically able to be a dynamic, reforming politician; but then that had never been his style. He radiated good will, common sense and fundamental decency, and he helped to keep the coalition together. He left the formulation of policies in other hands.

To admirers, Baldwin seemed a man of profound political skill. A young progressive Conservative backbencher in the 1930s, Harold Macmillan, later recalled in his memoirs the dominant political personality of the decade:

1 Baldwin had a unique hold on all sections of his party and the House as a whole. He was rarely attacked with any vigour, and if the House was excited or unruly he could usually and without difficulty reduce the temperature. His fairness in debate, the width and generosity of his
5 approach to life, the charm of his manner, and even the skilful way in which he could avoid a difficult argument or awkward situation by a few minutes of reminiscence or philosophising: all these qualities made him a superb Parliamentarian.

On the other hand, Baldwin's style did have its critics. A National Labour MP, Harold Nicolson, commented in his diary:

1 Baldwin makes one of his take-you-into-my-confidence speeches admitting that a mistake has been made. He says the time is past for platitudes and that we may now come back to stark realities. Yet he goes on with platitude after platitude, and by the end the House is no wiser
5 than before.

Ambitious young politicians sometimes found that Baldwin was not as helpful or as purposeful as they hoped. A junior minister described a meeting with him in 1935:

1 When you have explained your great plans to him, he will begin to tell you about some most interesting little book that he has just been reading, and will get up and run over all the shelves in his room till he finds it. Then he will talk about it again and eventually part from you without
5 having promised you any assistance, which in fact you will not get.

Baldwin can be seen as shrewd and politically aware or as a lazy and largely ineffectual individual, and perhaps these versions are simply two sides of the same coin. He was a great House of Commons man, sensitive to the moods of the backbenchers; he was also an effective orator who seemed to employ no oratory. But he was not a great policy-maker. In the national government he left that side of affairs to the man destined to succeed him as party leader and prime minister, Neville Chamberlain.

e) Neville Chamberlain

In the 1920s Neville Chamberlain had a record of domestic reform second to none. As Chancellor of the Exchequer in 1931–5, he spearheaded the formulation of policy on a wide variety of issues. Everyone recognised that eventually he would succeed to the premiership. The only question was when. In 1929 it had been put to him that he could successfully lead a revolt against Baldwin, but he had decided to remain loyal and not 'on any account play LG to his Asquith'. But sometimes the waiting got on his nerves, and in 1935, anxious for resignations, he wrote: 'I am more and more carrying this government on my back. The PM is ill and tired, Baldwin is tired and won't apply his mind to problems. It is certainly time there was a change.' Chamberlain was the strong man of the government, but he gave the impression of being humourless, intolerant and rather unapproachable, radiating efficiency but not warmth. Baldwin urged him – without success – not to give the impression that the looked on Labour as 'dirt'. He was far less concerned with consensus than was Baldwin.

2 Government Policies, 1931–5

> **KEY ISSUE** How successful were the National Government's policies?

a) The Economy and Unemployment

The national government was formed to combat the great depression. Between 1931 and 1935 economic issues had to be at the forefront of its concerns. There were four main features to the government's economic strategy. The first was the round of expenditure cuts imposed before the 1931 election – the 10 per cent reduction in unemployment benefit and government-controlled salaries; the second was the devaluation of the pound. Britain went off the gold standard in September 1931, and the pound fell in value by about 20 per cent compared with other currencies. This devaluation had been forced on the government, but soon the politicians began to realise the benefits of a 'weaker' pound. In particular, British exports were cheaper and therefore more competitive. The government then took deliberate action on the financial markets to keep the value of the pound down. The third strand to the financial strategy was a policy of low interest rates ('cheap money'). Interest rates were lowered from six per cent in 1931 to two per cent the following year and stayed at this level until 1939. This reduction encouraged the expansion of private enterprise, because the business community, as a rule, was more willing to borrow money when interest rates – and thus repayments – were low. The final policy was the one in which the Conservatives invested most of their energy and their hope – protection. Throughout the 1920s politicians had debated whether Britain should abandon free trade and introduce protection. Now a policy was implemented.

At the end of 1931 interim measures were taken: import duties could be imposed at short notice on goods that were entering the country in 'abnormal' quantities. Early the following year Neville Chamberlain steered the Import Duties Bill through parliament. This imposed a general duty of 10 per cent on all goods entering Britain, though goods from the British empire were to be exempt, pending an imperial conference to be held in Ottawa later in the year. It was the Import Duties Act which threatened the break-up of the coalition, but in the event the Liberal free-traders 'agreed to differ' with their protectionist colleagues. They argued that the act was not a final commitment to protection, as the imperial conference might substantially alter the policy. However, the free-traders felt they had no choice but to resign when the results of this conference were announced.

The Ottawa Conference of July and August 1932 was disappointing to those – like Beaverbrook, Chamberlain and the newly-converted Stanley Baldwin – who hoped that the empire would become a self-supporting economic unit, enjoying free trade within its component units but protected by tariff barriers against the rest of the world. Dominions like Canada and Australia feared that if the empire were free-trading, their own infant industries would suffer too much competition from British manufactured goods. Hence no common imperial economic policy emerged from the discussions. Instead there were 12 separate agreements, between Britain and the Dominions and between the Dominions themselves. The Dominions would not agree to empire free trade and they would not abolish tariffs against British goods: they merely decided to raise tariffs against non-British foreign items. Hence a measure of preference was given to imperial goods but not an effective measure, and most historians are agreed that Britain's tariff policy did little to aid the British economy. While it is true that during the rest of the 1930s Britain's trade was directed much more towards the empire, the overall level of trade was not boosted. The policy of which so much had been expected turned out to be of only marginal importance. In fact, the same has been said of the coalition's overall economic strategy. The government's measures probably neither helped nor hindered the British economy to any great extent. One distinguished historian, Robert

Blake, has commented that the extent to which government action contributed to recovery is 'anyone's guess'.

Britain pulled out of the depression, but only slowly. This is best illustrated by the unemployment totals. Unemployment remained at around 2.5 million from August 1931 to January 1933. Then it began to fall steadily. It was below 2 million in July 1935 and stood at 1.6 million after July 1936. The recovery was thus only partial and did not amount to a revival. As a result it is difficult to decide whether the government should be praised or blamed for its economic record. 'Cyclical' unemployment disappeared, but 'structural' employment remained. The staple industries of coal, textiles, iron and steel, and shipbuilding remained as depressed in the 1930s as in the 1920s. The national government made only a token effort to help the depressed areas. In 1935 the Special Areas Act made £2 million available to aid these parts of the country, but nothing substantial was achieved. About 44,000 workers were encouraged to move to other towns, and another 30,000 men were found places on retraining courses. The two commissioners who were responsible for implementing the legislation criticised its limitations and resigned in 1936. An amended Act appeared the following year. This tried to encourage firms to set up factories in the distressed areas, by offering remission of rates, rent and tax, up to 100 per cent for five years, but again little of substance was achieved.

The National Government did not directly attack the problem of unemployment. Its philosophy was summed up by *The Times* in 1932: 'the right way to deal with unemployment is to stimulate the normal activities of trade and industry.' Neville Chamberlain as Chancellor did not trust the new ideas stemming from Maynard Keynes (which had so influenced Lloyd George in 1929 and Oswald Mosley in 1930). Chamberlain did not believe that the government should attempt to employ men on large-scale public works, and felt that deficit financing and unbalanced budgets were unsound expedients; instead, attempts should be made to stimulate private enterprise. Perhaps he was right. Certainly in the mid-1930s capitalism did begin to boom and there were signs of real prosperity for those in work. 2.7 million houses were built in the 1930s, largely without any state subsidy. The numbers of cars on British roads doubled in the decade and the number of radios sold trebled. The first holiday camps appeared. The 1930s saw private affluence and the growth of new consumer goods industries, as well as unemployment and the hunger marches from Jarrow ('the town they killed') and elsewhere. By 1935 British industrial production was 11 per cent higher than in 1929, due to significant increases in productivity. Those in work were substantially better off, for whereas wage rates had fallen on average by three per cent since the start of the depression, the cost of living had fallen by almost 13 per cent.

It is probably true to say that Britain emerged from depression largely because of factors outside the government's control. By early-

1933 recovery began by itself. The revival of trade, on which the second Labour government had pinned its hopes, finally began to occur, and over the next few years the economy of most of the world began to improve. Another vital factor in British recovery was that people at home began to spend, to buy the new consumer goods that were available and thus to create a demand that fuelled employment. The government insisted that its economic policies were having a beneficial effect, but at the Exchequer Neville Chamberlain urged Britons to save rather than spend. He believed in the mistaken idea that medicine which is distasteful must be beneficial, and he helped to create a psychological climate that hindered expansion. Yet even the cautious Chamberlain agreed in 1934 and 1935 to restore the cuts in benefit and wages made in 1931.

Perhaps the national government erred on the side of caution. 'Safety first' was a motto which had been rejected by the electorate in 1929, but it was the unspoken watchword of the government nevertheless and it seemed to be approved by public opinion. Hence Chamberlain was able to devote his attention not to solving unemployment but to regularising the complex system of unemployment benefits. There were several anomalies, particularly the level of relief paid by different local authorities and the rigour with which they applied a means test. Chamberlain's answer was the Unemployment Act of 1934, an example of his forte – tidy-minded administrative reform. Insurance benefits were to apply for a maximum of 26 weeks. Those who were unemployed for longer and who claimed the dole – now termed 'unemployment assistance' – were to receive help, after a means test that applied to the whole household, according to national scales decided by a new and independent body, the Unemployment Assistance Board. The contentious issue of rates of benefit would thus be taken 'out of politics'. Yet in fact the government had to intervene when the UAB established rates that were so low that they caused public demonstrations.

b) India

In the early-1930s there was one issue which dominated parliamentary time more than any other – the future of India. In fact, debates on India in 1931–5 filled 4,000 printed pages of 'Hansard', the official record of parliamentary debates. Much less time was devoted to discussing the British economy. The basic problem for the government was how to reconcile their wish to retain control of India with the nationalists' demand to govern themselves. It was, said the Secretary of State for India, Sir Samuel Hoare, 'like trying to square the circle'. But no-one in the 1930s would admit that it was impossible.

Britain's policy towards India had been stated in 1917 and repeated in 1929: Britain would foster self-government in India so that eventually India would become a self-governing dominion, like

Australia or Canada. No longer would the self-governing parts of the Commonwealth be confined to former white-settler colonies. Although this was Britain's long-term aim, however, few British politicians believed that it should be achieved in the foreseeable future. The policy was in fact designed to appease the Indian National Congress, whose leader was Mahatma Gandhi and whose civil disobedience campaigns had disrupted British rule in the 1920s. The government hoped to give the Indians just enough power to buy their co-operation, but not so much that Britain's real control was lost. In other words, the government's apparent aim was to give the Indians more and more control over their own affairs, but its real motive was to hold on to the sub-continent. The head of the India Office had summed up Britain's attitude in the 1920s: 'If only we could go on doing nothing for a little longer.' But in the 1930s nationalist pressure had become too great to ignore. A series of important conferences was held in London, and Hoare was given the task of drawing up a new constitution that would satisfy both the British parliament, dominated by Conservatives, and Indian opinion.

In 1935 the Government of India Act became law. It was the longest act ever passed by a British parliament. Hoare had done well to overcome opposition in the Commons, headed by Winston Churchill. It was this issue of Indian reform which alienated Churchill from Tory leaders and kept him out of the National Government. As an old-fashioned imperialist, Churchill believed that nationalist pressure in India should be stoutly resisted. He told a friend that, in his opinion, Gandhi should be 'bound hand and foot at the gates of Delhi and trampled on by an enormous elephant ridden by the Viceroy'. In the Commons his language was more restrained, but he used his great parliamentary skill to delay the passage of the bill for as long as possible. As for Indian nationalists, they were not enthusiastic about the new constitution. Indians now had complete self-government in the provinces, but the central government was still under the control of the viceroy. India is still a prison, said Gandhi, 'but now there are a few more Indian warders'. The new act produced a lull in Anglo-Indian affairs, but the future was soon to see renewed confrontation.

c) Foreign Affairs

It was expected that in foreign affairs the government would have an easy time. The depression seemed likely to deepen the trend towards *détente*: nations would surely be too concerned with their domestic problems – and, to put it bluntly, too poor – for any expensive foreign adventures. This was indeed the case in Britain and France. There was a new inward-looking mood in Britain, and there were distinct signs that public opinion not only favoured peace but was pacifist. In 1933 a by-election took place at East Fulham. A Labour pacifist, fighting against a National Government candidate who favoured moderate rearmament, won a great victory when a government majority of over 14,000 was transformed into a Labour majority of nearly 5,000. In the same year Oxford undergraduates voted decisively not to fight for king and country. ('Can't row, won't fight' was Churchill's derisory comment on Oxford, which had recently lost the boat race against Cambridge.) Everyone realised that another war would be even more destructive than the last, given the advances in weapon technology. Baldwin summed up public fears with the words 'the bomber will always get through'.

In fact the depression had contrasting consequences. It made some countries more peaceful than ever; in others it undermined democracy and led dictators to favour war and foreign conquests, either as a means of acquiring new markets and raw materials and thus alleviating economic depression, or as a distraction from problems at home. The first aggressive action came from Japan, which invaded Manchuria in 1931 and set up a puppet state the following year. Britain supported a League of Nations investigation into the aggression, went along with the League's subsequent condemnation of Japan and then refused to recognise the new government in Manchuria. Yet few in Britain contemplated more vigorous action, especially at a time when the depression was at its height, and it was clear that the League had been successfully defied.

More worrying were events in Germany. In 1933 democracy collapsed and Adolf Hitler came to power. British politicians were slow to realise the menace posed by Hitler. He made no secret of the fact that he wished to see the Versailles settlement rewritten. But by this time most historians in Britain believed that the First World War had not been deliberately started by Germany, and it followed from this that the punitive Versailles treaty ought to be revised. Although Hitler's militarism gave some cause for concern, the British had become philosophically resigned to having to deal with all manner of foreign governments, most of which fell sadly short of British standards. The reassuring fact was that, in the short term at least, Hitler seemed powerless to cause much trouble because Germany was suffering from the depression even more than Britain. When Hitler came to power there were six million unemployed in Germany, and a German collapse seemed a more likely prospect than German resurgence.

Hitler's first foreign policy initiatives were low-key. He withdrew Germany from the League of Nations in October 1933. At the same time he pulled out of the world disarmament conference, but this body had been visibly moribund for several years. In January 1935, more menacingly, he introduced conscription. Britain's response was to begin a moderate rearmament programme of its own and to form the 'Stresa front' with France and

Italy. These three powers condemned Hitler's rearmament and announced that they would resist German aggression. The combined power of the Stresa nations seemed more than enough to deter Hitler, but in fact they could muster little unity. Within months the British annoyed the French by concluding a naval agreement with Germany which was contrary to the terms of the Treaty of Versailles, and the French alienated Britain by concluding a pact with the Soviet Union. But it was Italy which really disrupted the Stresa front. For years the Italian dictator Mussolini had dreamed of founding a new Roman Empire. Now he decided to attack one of the only two states in Africa that were not already ruled by Europeans, Abyssinia (present-day Ethiopia). In fact Mussolini prepared the ground for the invasion well. He had reason to believe that neither France nor Britain would destroy the Stresa front by complaining too loudly. He assumed that it would be in their interests to turn a blind eye, for Stresa disunity would open the way for German advances.

This was the situation in June 1935 when Baldwin finally took over as Prime Minister from MacDonald. At the same time Hoare, who was thought to have done well at the India Office, was promoted to become Foreign Secretary. It was clear that British public opinion had moved on since the supposed pacifism of 1933–4, and in particular the League of Nations was popular. Hoare decided that whatever qualms the government had about disrupting the Stresa front, the National Government should display their support of the League. In September he made a speech at the League's assembly in Geneva in favour of collective security. This received a 'rapturous reception' in Britain. In fact Hoare's reasoning was complicated and he did not feel committed to the League. He believed that if the League could be made into an effective instrument, all well and good, as sanctions could then be used against Italian and German aggressors. But he half-suspected that, whatever line Britain took, the League would be divided and at best half-hearted in imposing sanctions. In this case, while gaining credit for trying to work through the League, the government could return to the security offered by the Stresa front, even though this would mean conniving at Italian aggression in Africa.

The government was managing to gain prestige from the new crisis that was emerging in foreign affairs. The Labour party, on the other hand, was undergoing turmoil. At Labour's conference in October 1935 a policy supporting sanctions was adopted, despite the opposition of the leader of the party, the pacifist George Lansbury, who then resigned (see page 117). In the words of one historian, Labour committed *hari kiri*. A few days later Baldwin, who had been advised by Tory central office to hold a general election early the following year, seized on this golden opportunity and announced that a general election would be held on 14 November.

3 The General Election of November 1935

> **KEY ISSUE** Why did the National Government score another resounding victory?

When the economic depression became less severe, Baldwin had jus-tified the continuance of the coalition by pointing to the menace of right-wing dictatorships abroad and Labour's extremism at home. Now, at the end of 1935, he was able to call an election on these very issues. The atmosphere was very different from 1931. There was no sense of national panic or emergency, and it was clear that Labour would regain ground. But most political commentators assumed that the government would be returned with a substantial majority, which *The Times* predicted would be between 110 and 140 seats.

The election manifestos issued in 1935 attempted to win public support by making promises for future policy and also by judging that of the past. The National Manifesto (signed by Baldwin, MacDonald and Simon) insisted that the real issue for the electors:

1 is whether the stability and confidence which the National Government have built up are to be preserved in a period of special difficulty and anxiety ... The League of Nations will remain, as hereto-fore, the keystone of British foreign policy. The prevention of war and
5 the establishment of settled peace in the world must always be the most vital interest of the British people, and the League is the instru-ment which has been framed and to which we look for the attainment of these objects. We shall therefore continue to do all in our power to uphold the Covenant and to maintain and increase the efficiency of
10 the League ... The fact is that the actual condition of our defence forces is not satisfactory. We have made it clear that we must in the course of the next few years do what is necessary to repair the gaps in our defence, which have accumulated over the past decade ... The defence programme will be strictly confined to what is required to
15 make the country and the Empire safe, and to fulfil our obligations towards the League ... And we shall not for one moment relax our efforts to attain, by international agreement, a general limitation of armaments by every possible means ...

The remarkable fact that more persons are now employed in this
20 country than ever before in its history has not sprung from accident or the unfettered operation of natural laws. It has been the result of the deliberate policy of the Government in protecting the home market and in creating a regime of cheap money, which has facilitated enter-prise and stimulated industrial expansion ...
25 The advent of the Labour Opposition, pledged to a number of rev-olutionary measures of which the ultimate results could not be clearly foreseen, would inevitably be followed by a collapse of confidence ... The international situation reinforces the same lesson. The influence of

Britain among other nations, now so conspicuous, could never be main-
30 tained under an administration drawn from a party ... which is hope-
lessly divided on the most important points in foreign policy.

Labour's manifesto provided a complete contrast:

1 Four years have passed since the 'National' Government obtained a
swollen majority in the House of Commons on a campaign of fraud,
misrepresentation and panic ... At the end of four years the country
faces the grim spectacle of two million workless with an army of well
5 over a million and a half people on the Poor Law, and with the deep-
ening tragedy of the distressed areas ... The Government has robbed
the unemployed of benefit and subjected them to a harsh and cruel
household means test ...
   Whilst paying lip-service to the League it is planning a vast and
10 expensive re-armament programme, which will only stimulate similar
programmes elsewhere. The Government is a danger to the peace of
the world and to the security of this country ... Labour's policy calls for
a reversal of this suicidal foreign policy. It seeks wholehearted co-operation with the League of Nations and with all States outside the League
15 which desire peace ... Labour will efficiently maintain such defence
forces as are necessary and consistent with our membership of the
League; the best defence is not huge competitive national armaments,
but the organisation of collective security against any aggressor and the
agreed reduction of national armaments everywhere. Labour will pro-
20 pose to other nations the complete abolition of all national air forces,
the effective international control of civil aviation and the creation of an
international air police force; large reductions by international agreement in naval and military forces; and the abolition of private manufac-
ture of, and trade in, arms ...
25 At home, the Labour Party will pursue its policy of Socialist
Reconstruction. Labour has already put before the country, boldly and
clearly, schemes of public ownership for the efficient conduct, in the
national interest, of banking, coal and its products, transport, electricity,
iron and steel, and cotton ...

The election was marked by the use of election broadcasts on the
radio, where Baldwin was an effective performer. It was said that he
'has his feet on our fenders'. He claimed to understand the 'ordinary
working man' better than Labour, and many believed him. It has
been calculated that up to half of the electorate heard these broadcasts in 1935. Newsreel coverage of the campaign was also widely seen
in cinemas. The Conservatives did well in the local elections at the
start of November, and early on in the campaign Chamberlain
received favourable publicity for a promise that the government
would spend £100 million on road-building over the next five years.
Labour, on the other hand, had the embarrassing support of the
British Communist Party. The impression was soon confirmed that
the national government would be returned to office, although with

Party	General Election, 14 November 1935		
	No. of votes	Percentage of total votes	Seats
National Govt	11,755,654	53.7	432
Labour	8,325,491	37.9	154
Liberal	1,442,116	6.4	21

a reduced majority, and public interest flagged before election day. The popular newspapers turned their attention to the marriage of the Duke of Gloucester and a series of brutal murders. Turnout was five per cent lower than in 1931.

Labour gained 94 seats; but the government won the second highest percentage of the popular vote recorded in a general election since 1900. It was a comfortable and substantial victory for the national government – and, in reality, for the Conservatives, who won 388 seats out of the government's total of 432. Baldwin had a majority of around 250 over the other parties combined. No one realised it at the time, but in 1935 a parliament had been returned that was to survive for a decade.

4 The Abdication Crisis

KEY ISSUE Why was Edward VIII's reign so short?

It was not expected that Baldwin, now aged 68, would wish to remain active in politics for much longer. It also seemed, for a time, that he would retire under a cloud. In December 1935 Hoare, who had so recently spoken in support of the League of Nations and collective security, negotiated with the French Prime Minister, Pierre Laval, to buy off Mussolini, whose war with Abyssinia had now started. In return for ending the war, Mussolini was to be given two-thirds of Abyssinia, the Abyssinians being compensated by a strip of territory from British Somaliland that would give them access to the sea. But the plan was leaked to the newspapers and created a storm of disapproval in Britain. The scheme was disowned by Baldwin, who hastily sacked his Foreign Minister despite the fact that the whole cabinet had earlier approved his Abyssinian ideas. The League then imposed sanctions, although ineffectually, against Italy, destroying both the Stresa front and the credibility of the League as an instrument of collective security. Baldwin survived, but many felt that his image had been tarnished. In fact, when he eventually retired in 1937 he had never been more popular. The 'abdication crisis' restored his fortunes.

At the start of 1936 Baldwin had been feeling tired and run-down, and phosphorus pills had been prescribed by his doctor to combat nervous exhaustion. When a challenge emerged, however, the Prime

Minister rose to meet it. The problem was the new king, Edward VIII. George V, who had been a popular monarch, died in January 1936. Baldwin did not approve of his successor: Edward liked clothes that were too bright and patterns that were too large – he even had turn-ups on his trousers. He had also made statements that seemed too sympathetic to the unemployed. More seriously, he seemed too friendly towards Nazi Germany. Indeed the head of MI6 told Baldwin that the contents of secret documents which had been leaked to the Germans had been traced back to the King. Soon it was decided that certain papers should not be shown to Edward. But the most important of all the charges against the king was that he proposed to marry an American divorcee, Mrs Wallis Simpson.

Edward was 40 and a bachelor. The British monarch was supposed to provide an example of respectability for the nation, but the new king had had several 'friendships' with married women in the past (including an affair that lasted 16 years with the wife of one of the Liberal whips), and now he was consorting with Mrs Simpson (who, it was rumoured, having been brought up in 'much seduced circumstances', had learned the arts of love in a Chinese brothel). The problem only became acute in October 1936 when she obtained a divorce from her husband (on the grounds of his adultery with the improbably named Buttercup Kennedy). The King informed the Prime Minister that he wished to marry her. A crisis had arisen. Baldwin considered the marriage impossible for several reasons: Mrs Simpson was an American, she was a commoner and she had been twice divorced – making a mockery of the marriage ceremony which was supposed to unite people 'til death did them part, words which the king, as 'supreme governor' of the Church of England, should take seriously. Baldwin made it clear that he was not talking merely for himself, but for the British people as a whole – whereupon Edward retorted that he spoke as if he were a Gallup Poll. If the King ignored his Prime Minister's advice and married, a full-scale constitutional crisis would erupt. Edward was king not only of Great Britain but of the Dominions, and there was a real possibility that Canada (the most puritanical part of the empire) would cut its links with Britain if Mrs Simpson were queen. Also, the British government would resign if the Prime Minister's advice were ignored and action would be taken to alter the monarch's place in the constitution. The survival of the monarchy would have been in doubt.

The country was more deeply divided than Baldwin possibly realised. The King had his supporters, although whether they did his cause much good is doubtful. These, known as the 'cavaliers', included Lord Beaverbrook, Winston Churchill, Britain's fascist leader Sir Oswald Mosley and the leader of the British Communist Party. However, Baldwin impressed upon the King that his real choice was between giving up Mrs Simpson and abdication; in the end Edward chose the latter. In December 1936 he gave up the throne for 'the woman I love'. He was succeeded by his younger brother, who became George VI. Despite shyness and a stutter, George carried on where his father had left off, and the monarchy suffered no long-term damage from the crisis.

Baldwin remained premier long enough to see the new King enthroned and then retired in May 1937. Everyone agreed that he had handled the abdication crisis well. *The Times* insisted that 'in handling a great national problem ... he has no comparable rival'. Historians have also praised the skill he displayed in a crisis that certainly could have got out of hand. But Edward VIII was the man who really solved the problem: had he been resolved to remain monarch and to marry Mrs Simpson, Baldwin's actions might seem much less impressive. As Beaverbrook commented to Churchill, 'Our cock won't fight'.

5 The Political Significance of Stanley Baldwin

KEY ISSUE What did Baldwin achieve?

Stanley Baldwin dominated interwar British politics to a greater extent than any other individual. He certainly enjoyed his fair share of luck – in his appointment as prime minister in 1923, in surviving the electoral setbacks that produced two Labour governments, and in the formation of a coalition in 1931 which allowed him to tame his right wing. Some believe that luck dominated his whole career; indeed he has been depicted by several historians as a lazy man of mediocre abilities, with no major legislative achievement or reform to his credit, who did his country a disservice by keeping out of office men of real talent. However, luck alone cannot explain his success. He also showed profound skill. Churchill called him 'the most formidable politician I have ever encountered in public life'. (Perhaps not the least of Baldwin's shrewd judgements was his view that Churchill might be needed as a future war leader.)

Baldwin has been called 'an artist in politics', a man of extreme political sensitivity with an uncanny ability to judge the mood of the nation. Certainly he was capable of astute political judgement, and it was he, more than anyone else, who kept the Conservatives united in the interwar years. Yet he also seemed a man above party politics. He was no bigoted partisan. He always looked for common ground, for consensus, and he did much to convince the electorate that politicians could be trusted. He would even admit making mistakes and gain credit for this candour. He was not a man of great energy or stamina. He was inclined to sit on the fence, to look before leaping and then to decide not to leap. He did not possess the originality, the mental agility or the oratorical skills of Lloyd George, but occasionally he could speak with an eloquence that stemmed from deep conviction and on the radio he was extremely effective. It was characteristic that he should be associated with no particular policy or reform, but arguably his success was no less marked for this. The personal trust that many felt for Baldwin helped democracy to function in Britain when it was failing elsewhere. One working man, seeing Baldwin on film in the 1935 election campaign, commented: 'What I likes about Baldwin, 'e don't sling no mud.' His was the voice of moderation and decency. He was the most highly trusted and respected prime minister this century. He was not spectacular, exciting or energetic, but he cleverly made a virtue out of what he lacked, and his unconcern with the details of government allowed him to achieve a sense of perspective. Baldwin has had many admirers and many critics. What no one should deny is that he came close to embodying British democracy – with both its weaknesses and its strengths – in the 1920s and 1930s.

6 Neville Chamberlain and Appeasement

> **KEY ISSUE** Why did Chamberlain attempt to appease Hitler?

Chamberlain became Prime Minister in May 1937. He was the obvious choice to succeed Baldwin, and in many ways he was the only choice. Perhaps the premiership had come too late for him, as he was 68 and only two years younger than Baldwin. But he was still vigorous and, despite the fact that the 'national' government was now little more than a Conservative front, the government under his guidance continued to pursue domestic policies of moderate reform. In 1937 the Factory Act raised minimum standards of safety at work, and added 4 million workers to the 7 million already covered by its provisions. The government also increased the scope of old-age and widows' pensions legislation, encouraged an extension of holidays with pay in industry, and embarked on a programme of slum clearance. In 1938 the Coal Mines Act nationalised mining royalties, and the following year the government set up a public corporation, the British Overseas Airways Corporation (BOAC), to dominate the British civil aviation industry. As in the 1920s, the Conservatives saw a place for state control and direction in the economy.

Chamberlain would have liked to devote much more time to such reasonable and progressive reforms. Unfortunately, he had to deal with the menacing international situation. A revived Nazi Germany was threatening the peace of Europe. Already in March 1936, when the international gaze was focused on the war in Abyssinia, Hitler had sent troops into the Rhineland, which Germany had agreed under the Locarno Treaty to keep permanently demilitarised. Now he let it be known that he wanted to see further changes, including the union between Germany and Austria and the incorporation of all Germans within Germany, including those in Czechoslovakia and Poland. This claim to national self-determination was not the limit of Hitler's ambition. It was merely a first step – but a skilful one, for he was playing on the sense of guilt that many in Britain felt. Chamberlain and others in the government thought that Hitler's grievances were essentially reasonable. After all, if, as people were convinced, Germany had not deliberately caused the First World War, the Treaty of Versailles had been unfair and the Germans were quite right to complain at the way they had been treated. Under Chamberlain, Britain's policy was appeasement – the attempt to satisfy Hitler's aspirations by agreement and compromise, thus avoiding war. In fact, this had been Britain's basic aim under MacDonald and Baldwin, but under Chamberlain it was pursued much more actively.

In March 1938 Hitler's troops moved unopposed into Austria, which was then annexed and became a province of Germany. Britain's response has been described by one historian as 'apologetic indignation'. Then Hitler began to protest at the position of the German minority in the Sudetenland of Czechoslovakia. He said he was prepared to go to war in order to rescue his German compatriots. It was on this issue that Chamberlain took the initiative and acted as peacemaker. He flew to meet Hitler three times to mediate, and on the third occasion, at Munich in September 1938, a deal was struck which prevented war. Hitler was given the whole of the Sudetenland, despite the fact that this area was vital to Czechoslovakian defences and economic prosperity. It was very much like the Hoare-Laval plan, although the Munich agreement was not disowned by the British public. In fact, Chamberlain received a remarkable reception on his return to Britain. He had never been a popular figure before, but now, briefly, he was a hero. 'Praise be to God and to Mr Chamberlain,' wrote one journalist; 'I see no blasphemy in coupling those two names.' It was, the Prime Minister said with naive optimism, 'peace in our time'. Six months later Hitler invaded the remainder of Czechoslovakia, occupying territory to which he had no legitimate claim whatsoever. Hitler stood exposed as an unprincipled aggressor, and Chamberlain decided to try to deter him: he guaranteed Poland, while at the same time putting pressure on the Poles to make some concessions to Germany. But on 1 September Hitler's troops invaded Poland, and two days later Britain declared war on Germany.

Appeasement did not work. Hitler was not appeased – indeed he was not appeasable, for he looked upon concessions as weakness and respected only strength. A suitable epitaph on Chamberlain's policy was provided in the House of Commons: the Prime Minister, it was said, had 'eaten dirt in vain'. Yet the policy of appeasement was not a product, as many once assumed, of fear and stupidity. Chamberlain was acutely aware of Britain's economic and defence weaknesses, of her lack of allies, and of the fact that a war between Britain and

Germany would leave the British empire vulnerable to attacks from the Japanese and the Italians. Many of the historians who have studied appeasement in depth have concluded that Chamberlain had very good reasons for his actions and that appeasement was a 'natural' policy for him to pursue, given the difficult circumstances of the time. It has also been pointed out, in Chamberlain's own words, that while 'hoping for the best' he was also 'preparing for the worst'. He rearmed, in case appeasement did not work – not an all-out, crash programme of rearmament, which might have inflicted real harm on the British economy, but rearmament which targeted funds to fighter planes and radar defence, both of which proved of inestimable worth in the Battle of Britain in 1940. He has been praised for his sense of realism and for delaying Britain's entry into the war until a time when the British people were united and when Britain had the moral support of neutral nations like the United States.

Chamberlain's policy of appeasement is one of the most hotly contested topics in modern British history, and one of the most fascinating. There seem to be more pro-Chamberlainites these days, but his critics point out that Chamberlain was perhaps an unconscious pacifist who had to be forced by a backbench revolt into declaring war on 3 September. Evidence is also accumulating that his government, instead of following British public opinion or trying to educate the public to a better understanding of Hitler, deliberately censored the media and tried to create a dishonestly favourable image of Nazi Germany. Appeasement may well have become an obsession with Chamberlain, a matter of blind faith.

Whatever verdict is reached about the merits of appeasement, there can be no doubt that foreign policy was the most vital factor affecting British politics from 1937 onwards. Gradually the Labour party decided on a firmer policy towards Hitler. In 1937 Labour MPs abandoned their practice of voting against defence expenditure and abstained instead, and in the following year they were in favour of increased armaments. But in April 1939 their leader came out against conscription. The significant alternatives to Chamberlain emerged not among the opposition but within the Conservative party.

a) Opposition to Chamberlain

Chamberlain's political style contrasted to Baldwin's. The new Prime Minister dominated his ministers and was particularly determined to control foreign policy. No prime minister was less under the influence of his civil servants or foreign secretary. In fact he achieved far more personal control of his government than Lloyd George had managed after the First World War. It was said that Lloyd George had used Curzon as the 'gilded doormat' after 1918; now Chamberlain used his Foreign Secretary, Anthony Eden – the handsome MP for Warwick who had become Foreign Secretary in 1935 at the age of only

38 – as a glamorous doormat. Eden was known to be more anti-Italian than his Prime Minister, but his main complaint was simply that he was not consulted enough. In February 1938 he resigned and soon become a focus for MPs discontented with Chamberlain's appeasement.

The other focus for criticism in the Tory party was Churchill. He put himself forward as the chief anti-appeaser and made extensive criticisms of Chamberlain. On the Prime Minister's return from Munich, for example, he told him that he had been 'given a choice between war and dishonour. You chose dishonour, but you will still have war'. Churchill was to be vindicated by events, but for a long time he seemed to damn the cause of anti-appeasement by espousing it. People were very suspicious of Churchill. His attitude towards India had branded him a reactionary, and some thought he was too much of a fascist himself. Certainly he seemed to lack sound judgement, and it was widely believed that he was a warmonger. After Munich, there were about 30 Conservative dissenters – the 'Old Guard' (centred on Churchill) and the 'Glamour Boys' (centred on Eden). It was Eden's group which attracted more support, despite the fact that his views were more ambiguous than those of Churchill. It was also Eden who seemed a more acceptable leader to those members of the Labour party who wished to form an anti-Chamberlain front.

b) War

On 3 September 1939 Britain declared war on Germany. Chamberlain stated, quite accurately: 'Everything that I have worked for, everything that I have hoped for, everything that I have believed in during my public life has crashed into ruins.' Yet in fact his political position was still secure, and the overwhelming majority of Conservative MPs in the Commons still supported him. The national mood was very different in 1939 from 1914, being grim and sober, but on both occasions it seemed that war need produce little political change in Britain. Chamberlain invited Churchill and Eden to join the government, but otherwise things continued as before. Few could have guessed at the political transformation that the war would bring.

Summary Diagram
The National Government, 1931–9

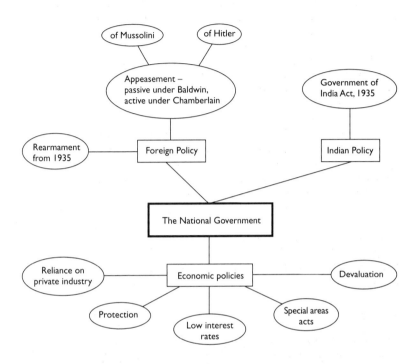

You need a detailed set of notes on this chapter. The chapter headings and sub-headings should provide useful guidance. Try to make up your own mind on the key issues: 1) MacDonald's career, expanding the section on his achievements by using earlier parts of the book; 2) Baldwin's career, explaining his long political survival; 3) the 1935 election, using your knowledge of events from 1931 to 1935 to explain why so many voted for the National Government; and 4) appeasement, engaging with the 'for' and 'against' interpretations

Answering essay questions on Chapter 5

Many aspects of this topic can appear on examination papers. The roles of Baldwin and/or Chamberlain may be highlighted, but perhaps the most typical question is:

1. Account for the dominance of the Conservative Party in domestic British politics from 1931 to 1939.

Construct a first paragraph. Remember the importance of explaining as clearly as possible the meaning of the question and defining its terms. In particular, you will have to comment on the issue of whether they were dominant and, if so, to what extent. Does the question imply that the national government was just a Tory facade? Would you mention the elections of 1931 and 1935? Which reasons for their success would you mention? The economic recovery? The popularity of appeasement? The weakness of the opposition groups? Will you mention the three key individuals for the decade (Baldwin, MacDonald and Chamberlain)? Would you highlight one factor as the pre-eminent reason for Conservative dominance? Could Baldwin be the major factor?

Once you are satisfied with this paragraph, draw up a plan for the rest of the essay. You should in fact be expanding the opening section: the views you expressed at the beginning should be consistently held, and the important areas identified at the beginning should be expanded into paragraphs. (Next, alter the dates to make a different question: account for Conservative dominance from 1918 to 1939. This is another very popular issue. Repeat the exercises of writing a first paragraph and then sketching an essay plan.)

Another question worth considering is:

2. 'A domestic record of complete failure.' Do you agree with this verdict on the National Government?

Attempt another essay plan. Remember the vital importance of breaking down the government's domestic work into separate categories. (In other words, write your own 'structured question'. What smaller questions would you choose?) Remember the obvious – that you have to answer the question. Do you agree with the quotation? If you see any element of even partial success in any aspect of the government's domestic record, then obviously you do not.

Source-based questions on Chapter 5

1. Ramsay MacDonald on National Labour
Read the extract on page 91 and answer the following questions:

a) What might MacDonald have meant by saying that National Labour would be 'neither red, white nor blue'? (*2 marks*)

b) Does it seem from the extract that the National Labour group had any distinguishing features? Explain your answer. (*4 marks*)

c) What impression of MacDonald is the author trying to convey? (*4 marks*)

2. *Three views of Baldwin*
Read the extracts on page 94, and answer the following questions:

a) Do you accept the view that Baldwin had a unique hold on 'all sections of his party' (line 1)? Explain your answer. (*4 marks*)

b) What qualities does the author imply are the marks of a 'superb Parliamentarian' (line 9)? (*4 marks*)

c) Do you find the second extract (lines 1–5) a convincing attack on Baldwin? Explain your answer. (*5 marks*)

d) What does the third extract (lines 1–5) tell us of Baldwin's political style? What additional information would you wish to know about this meeting in making your judgement? (*6 marks*)

e) Comment on the reliability of each of the extracts in terms of the likely bias of their authors. (*6 marks*)

3. *The National and Labour 1935 Manifestos*
Read the extracts on pages 102–03, and answer the following questions:

a) Examine the sections dealing with foreign policy in each of the manifestos (page 102 lines 3–19 and page 103 lines 9–25). Comment on their differences in content and emphasis. (*7 marks*)

b) Examine the sections on the economic record of the national government (page 102 lines 20–5 and page 103 lines 5–8). Which of the two analyses do you find the more historically accurate? Why? (*7 marks*)

c) How far does the Labour manifesto justify the charges made against Labour in the final paragraph of the National manifesto? (*5 marks*)

d) Using the extracts and your wider knowledge, explain how far the policies in the manifestos influenced the results of the 1935 general election. (*11 marks*)

6 Opposition in the 1930s

POINTS TO CONSIDER

This chapter considers the opposition parties in parliament in the 1930s and also the undemocratic groups, both fascist and communist. You have to estimate their strength, understand the challenges they posed and decide why those challenges failed. Most difficult of all, you have to try to see them in perspective in order to assess their significance.

KEY DATES

1920 Founding of the Communist Party of Great Britain (CPGB).
1921 Founding of the National Unemployed Workers' Movement (NUWM) by Wal Hannington.
1932 Cripps founded the Socialist League; (1 Oct.) Mosley launched the British Union of Fascist (BUF).
1934 (7 June) BUF rally at Olympia: violence led to withdrawal of Rothermere's support; (Nov.) Labour gained control of the London County Council.
1935 (Oct.) Lansbury resigned as Labour's leader and was replaced by Attlee.
1936 Left Book Club was formed; (4 Oct.) Battle of Cable Street; (Dec.) Public Order Act, banning political uniforms.
1939 (August) Nazi–Soviet Pact; (Sept.) outbreak of Second World War.
1940 (May) Arrest of Oswald Mosley.

The national government dominated parliamentary politics after its landslide victory in the 1931 general election. As a result, while many other nations in Europe were plunged into turmoil, Britain achieved profound political stability for the rest of the decade. Yet, paradoxically, the 1930s also saw significant political volatility. The Liberals continued their headlong decline into political insignificance, while Labour reacted constructively to the new political scene. But there was also a real challenge to the existing order from the extreme left and the extreme right. British communists and fascists, however, appealed for support not so much in parliament as on the streets.

1 The Liberals

KEY ISSUE How did the Liberals fare after 1931?

The story of the Liberal party in the 1930s is one of electoral disaster. After the election of 1931, in which the party was starved of money and candidates, the Liberals were split three ways: Samuelites, Simonites and Lloyd George's tiny following. The divisions were not healed, and for the rest of the decade the decline continued. There was a fall in the number of candidates the party put forward at elections and a decline in their electoral successes. In 1929 12.5 per cent of candidates at the general election had been Liberals, in 1931 the figure was below 10 per cent and in 1935 it stood at below eight per cent. In 1931 the Liberals won one in seven council seats, but by 1935 they won only one in ten. The party also had a very poor record at by-elections. In the 1935 general election Liberals won only 21 seats (not counting the Simonites who, as members of the national government, were indistinguishable from Conservatives). The Liberals became increasingly irrelevant to British politics and their votes were captured by either Labour or Conservatives.

2 The Labour Party

> **KEY ISSUE** How did Labour manage to recover from the debacle of 1931?

The general election of 1931 was a traumatic shock for Labour. It was as if the natural course of history had been altered: the 'inevitability of gradualness' had been disrupted. 'The one thing that is not inevitable now,' commented one Labour MP, 'is gradualness.' No longer, it seemed, was the success of socialism guaranteed. From being the largest single party in 1929, Labour had been reduced overnight to only 52 MPs. Labour's leader, Arthur Henderson, was defeated, and so were 12 other former cabinet ministers. The sole surviving cabinet minister from the rout, the 72-year old George Lansbury, became leader by default. Labour did equally badly at the municipal elections in November 1931, and in five by-elections the following year the party did not put forward a single candidate, mainly because it could not afford to. It was suffering a financial crisis. All the staff at Transport House, Labour's headquarters, were forced to accept a five per cent cut in salaries. It seemed that Labour might follow the Liberals into decline.

From 1933 onwards, however, there was an upturn in Labour's fortunes, as well as the generation of fresh ideas in important policy debates. Despite its spectacular defeat in the general election of 1931, Labour had retained a healthy share of the popular vote. The proportional representation society put Labour's performance into perspective: under PR, Labour would have won 225 seats in 1929 (as opposed to 288), and 168 in 1931 (as opposed to 52). 30.6 per cent of the total vote was a strong base on which to build – and build Labour did. There were important improvements to the party's organisation. A by-election insurance fund was started in 1933, to subsidise the election expenses of poorer constituencies, and in the same year a membership drive recruited 100,000 new party members. As a result, 10 seats were won at by-elections before 1935 and the party did exceptionally well at local elections, capturing control of the London County Council for the first time in 1934.

These years also saw important debates on policies within Labour ranks. Labour was still a very 'broad church' and there was no unanimity in the way sections of the party reacted to defeat in 1931. There was a tendency to lay all the blame on MacDonald and the other defectors to the national government, and trade union leaders in particular saw little reason for self-examination or fundamental changes in party policy. But other, more self-critical elements called for a reappraisal. After the experience of 1929–31, the party agreed that it would never again form a minority administration and that once in office it would introduce 'definite socialist legislation immediately'. A policy sub-committee was set up at the end of 1931 which soon recommended the nationalisation of key sectors of the economy. However, other ideas, put forward by the Socialist League, were not generally accepted within the party.

The Socialist League was founded by Sir Stafford Cripps in 1932. Cripps, a rather puritanical vegetarian as well as a successful barrister from a wealthy and privileged background, had been Solicitor-General in the second Labour government and had managed to hold on to his seat at the general election. Under his guidance the League proposed to abolish the House of Lords and to nationalise the means of production within five years, with full workers' control of industry:

1 If we are to witness a change in the economic and social structure of the country, such as we believe to be essential to prosperity, it is clear that such a change can never be brought about under the existing Parliamentary forms ... One factor in the change is of vital importance.
5 A change so fundamental cannot take place unless the Government of the country is assured of the support of those who hold the economic, as distinct from the political, power. We must face the fact that those who at present hold the economic power will refuse their support to any Labour government. The idea that if the Labour Party is gentle and
10 well-behaved, it will persuade the capitalists to hand over their economic power to the government is quite fantastic ... Continuity of policy, even in fundamentals, can find no place in a socialist programme. It is this complete severance with all traditional theories of government, this determination to seize power from the ruling class and transfer it
15 to the people, that differentiates the present political struggle from all those that have gone before.

Cripps therefore advocated that a future Labour government would have to pass an emergency powers act to prevent the capitalists sabotaging socialism. This legislation would extend the life of parliament beyond the normal five years and allow rule by ministerial decree. But his views were too theoretical and extreme for the bulk of Labour supporters. Beatrice Webb described Cripps as 'oddly immature in intellect and unbalanced in judgement', and many found him arrogant. Churchill was later to comment: 'There, but for the grace of God, goes God.'

In 1935, when the key political question of the day was whether the League of Nations should impose sanctions against aggressors, Cripps judged that warfare and the imposition of sanctions were both capitalist plots designed ultimately to increase private profit. Labour's leader George Lansbury also opposed sanctions, but from Christian principles. Lansbury insisted that he would 'close every recruiting station, disband the army, and disarm the air force. I would abolish the whole dreadful equipment of war and say to the world "Do your worst".' Lansbury was a great favourite with the delegates at Labour's conference in October 1935, but even so his pacifist policy was defeated. Lansbury resigned and was replaced as leader by Clement Attlee. The new man was described by one newspaper as 'a good enough parliamentarian, but desperately uninspiring'. Churchill called him 'a sheep in sheep's clothing'. The most fundamental lesson Labour learned from the crisis of 1931 was that henceforth the leader of the party must be controlled by the party. It has been said, with much justice, that Labour's most influential figure for a generation after 1931 was 'the ghost of Ramsay MacDonald'.

In many ways Attlee had earned the leadership. He had been an MP since 1922 and had served as a junior minister in the second Labour government. He had worked as an industrious assistant to Lansbury, deputising for him when he broke a hip, and had accumulated seniority in the party. But he was an uncharismatic, rather self-effacing man, who seemed less dynamic than his rivals in 1935, one of whom wrote after the party election that now a 'nonentity ... a little mouse' was to be leader. In fact these qualities were Attlee's major attractions, as he would not dominate and disrupt the party as MacDonald had done. He attracted no fervent support and he was no orator. With Attlee as leader, policies not personalities would spearhead the party's appeal. Also with this moderate leader, 'extreme' policies would be debated but not acted upon.

After 1935 Cripps and the Socialist League called for Labour to allow Communist affiliation and for a 'popular front' or 'united front' between all groups on the left and in the centre opposed to the government and its policy of appeasement. But the party leadership would have none of it. There was an efflorescence of ideas on the left, but the Labour party under Attlee continued to tread the path of parliamentary moderation and of evolutionary, as opposed to revolutionary, socialism. Gradually the party abandoned its pacifist tendencies and began to support rearmament and a firmer line against Hitler (see page 109), but Cripps was repudiated. In March 1939 he and several supporters were expelled from the party. At the annual conference that year one trade unionist delegate insisted that Labour was better off without 'cranks ... and their damned -isms ... Away with those senseless females and those ladylike young gentlemen who waste their time advocating everything from the establishment of nudist colonies to pensions for indigent cats.' The party had regained its confidence. Labour was committed to fostering democratic socialism and would not be associated with ideas like communism, revolution or pacifism. MacDonald was hated by all on the left; yet there is much truth in the idea that his vision of the Labour party was gradually being realised.

At the 1935 election Labour did very respectably, winning 154 seats and gaining a higher percentage of the total vote (37.9) than ever before in its history. The party was still a long way from power, given the national government's substantial victory, but Labour was a growing political force in Britain. Before the start of the Second World War a dozen more seats were won at by-elections. It has even been argued that, had a general election been held in 1940, Labour might have won, and certainly they could have expected to do much better than in 1935. By the end of the interwar period the 1931 crisis was no more than a bitter memory, and Labour had successfully put its own house in order.

3 The Extreme Left

> **KEY ISSUE** How serious a challenge was mounted by Communism in the 1930s?

a) The Communist Party

The Communist Party of Great Britain (CPGB) had been set up in 1920 to bring about a workers' revolution. There seemed little likelihood of early success and, on Lenin's advice, the party attempted to co-operate with Labour. But to Labour, this seemed less like co-operation than infiltration – and with good reason, for Lenin insisted that the communists would 'support Henderson as a rope supports a man who is hanged'. Communist affiliation was rejected three times in the early-1920s by a Labour party anxious to appear respectable in the eyes of the voters, and in 1925 Labour insisted that individual members of the Communist party were ineligible to join the Labour party. Moscow then shifted its position and insisted that there could be no co-operation with bourgeois, opportunist and doctrinally unsound social democratic parties. Yet by the end of the decade the

Communists in Britain had only around 3,000 members, half of whom were in the mining areas of South Wales and Scotland. In the 1929 election 25 Communist candidates polled no more than 56,000 votes in total (an average of little over 2,000 per candidate), and the Communists were 'a revolutionary party in a non-revolutionary situation'.

The great depression was decidedly to the Communists' advantage, as the end of capitalism seemed to be at hand. In 1931 party membership doubled, but in the election of that year 26 candidates received a total of only 75,000 votes. Nevertheless, in 1932 membership grew to 9,000 and as high as 16,000 by the end of 1938. The CPGB was behind a number of strikes, including the Lancashire cotton strike in 1932, and its newspaper, the *Daily Worker*, had a circulation of about 80,000. Communist ideology appealed to a number of middle-class intellectuals: a bevy of spies was recruited at Cambridge (including Philby, Burgess, Maclean and Blunt) and several poets (including W.H. Auden and C. Day Lewis) nailed the red flag to their mast. But there was little hope of communism succeeding unaided in Britain. Communists achieved influential positions within the South Wales miners' union, but most workers remained committed to Labour and most of the unemployed seemed politically apathetic. ('There's no mob any more,' complained Orwell, 'only a flock.') The depression had not produced the 'revolutionary situation' that the extreme left had hoped for.

From 1933 onwards Moscow ordered a change of tactics: British Communists were to join with other left-wing groups to stem the rise of fascism in Europe. Hence at the general election of 1935, the CPGB put forward only two candidates – one of whom was in fact elected – and encouraged its supporters to vote Labour. An MP from South Wales urged that Communist affiliation to the Labour party would lead to the 'spiritual awakening' of the whole working-class movement, but Labour once again voted decisively against the proposal at its annual conference in 1936. The popular front movement had appeal to Cripps and the Socialist League – and in November 1938 a popular front candidate won a spectacular by-election victory – but was condemned by Labour's leaders. Hitler's Germany seemed a menace, but Stalin's Russia seemed scarcely more attractive. A series of 'show trials' in the mid-1930s, in which Stalin's potential enemies were executed after confessing to imaginary crimes, was endorsed by the British Communist Party ('Shoot the Reptiles' was a headline in the *Daily Worker*); but to Labour's moderate leaders the executions were a dire warning against too close an involvement with the Soviet Union or the CPGB.

Communist influence certainly made itself felt in the realm of ideas, as shown by the success of the Left Book Club, which was set up in 1936. One year later it had 50,000 members, to whom were sold the two 'books of the month' selected by its editors. Over half of the books issued in its first year were written by Communists. By the end of 1937 the club had 730 local discussion groups, attended on average by 12,000 people every fortnight. There were even groups meeting abroad, from Norway to Chile. The outbreak of the Spanish Civil War in 1936 added to the ferment of ideas which the club encouraged. General Franco, seen as a fascist by Hitler and Mussolini, led a military coup against a popular front republican government which was falling increasingly under communist influence. Spain was the scene of the physical battles; but Britain was part of the wider, ideological battlefield. British communists organised an 'Aid Spain' campaign. Yet the Left Book Club literature may have been a substitute for action rather than a preparation for it – a harmless 'letting off of steam'. Labour's leaders certainly disliked it, and it did not generate any significant communist enthusiasm among the majority of the public.

A crushing blow to the Communist party came in August 1939. Germany and Russia signed the Nazi-Soviet Pact. Once again the CPGB was ordered to reverse its policy: fascism was no longer the enemy, because Germany was an ally of the Soviet Union. The popular front was to be hastily jettisoned. This was too much for all but the most faithful and obedient supporters in Britain, and communism was eclipsed by the mood of patriotism which Britain's entry into the war produced.

b) The National Unemployed Workers' Movement

A more significant left-wing body, and certainly a more proletarian one, was the National Unemployed Workers' Movement (NUWM) which was set up in 1921 by Wal Hannington, one of the founder members of the CPGB. Inaugurated to agitate for 'work or full maintenance', it had achieved little in the 1920s but was boosted by the onset of the depression in 1929. In 1929 it had 10,000 members; by 1932 it had 50,000. Special Branch kept close and hostile scrutiny of the Movement, and both the Labour party and the TUC distanced themselves from it.

The NUWM did much to publicise the plight of the unemployed, organising campaigns against cuts in benefit and against the means test. 'Hunger marches' to London were undertaken. In October 1932, for example, 18 separate marches, involving 2,000 people, met up in London to present a million-signature petition against the means test. A rally in Hyde Park attracted tens of thousands of supporters, but the petition was not presented. Scuffles broke out, 2,000 police intervened and Hannington was arrested and sentenced to three months' imprisonment. In 1934 a similar, though more orderly, march was organised, but the Prime Minister refused to see a delegation of workers. In 1935 the Movement organised demonstrations against the low rates of benefit instituted by the Unemployment

Assistance Board (see page 98); this time they had more success, and the scale of benefits was raised. The NUWM also staged stunts to attract publicity: a group of unemployed men demanded tea at the Ritz; a 30-foot banner was unfurled at the top of the Monument in the City of London. But after 1935, as the depression eased and a substantial number of people began to enjoy signs of affluence, the Movement ceased to be important.

Despite the worries of the police, the NUWM had not become a real mass movement: it never attracted more than a tiny proportion of the unemployed, it had difficulty surviving financially and its leader, Wal Hannington, was in prison three times in the 1930s. Nor did it lead to a breakdown in law and order, although there certainly were several violent clashes with police. In Liverpool and Birkenhead in September 1932 an anti-means test demonstration turned into a riot, after which over 40 people were taken to hospital. The following month, in Belfast, police opened fire on demonstrators, killing two. Yet the protests had been of a limited character: damages in the worst year, 1932, were estimated by police at a mere £200, mostly for broken windows (one of which alone had cost £120).

In retrospect, it seems that the most useful work performed by Hannington was not his organisation of hunger marches or his campaigns for communism but his expert advice to the unemployed about the benefits they were entitled to claim. He was an expert on the complex and ever-changing regulations that governed unemployment benefit. Under his direction the NUWM fought more than 2,000 legal cases over denial of benefit and was successful in more than a third of them. Certainly, neither the NUWM nor communism in general mounted a significant challenge to the government in the 1930s. Communism never became more than a marginal movement. Perhaps its greatest success lay in opposing another, and in some ways similar, minority movement – British fascism.

4 Mosley and the British Union of Fascists

> **KEY ISSUE** Why did fascism fail in Britain?

a) Origins and Ideology

The most significant challenge to British parliamentary democracy in the 1930s came from Sir Oswald Mosley, who in 1932 set up the British Union of Fascists (BUF). Historians used to argue that fascism was completely alien to British traditions, that Mosley himself was simply 'a highly gifted playboy' who was playing at being a dictator and had no real staying power, and that support for the BUF peaked at 20,000 members and declined because of timely action by the

British government. Fascism could thus be seen as an isolated episode in the 1930s, with no connections with the past or the future. Fascism was somehow alien to the British character, so that 'British fascism' was almost a contradiction in terms and Mosley's movement was doomed to failure from the start. However, recent research has modified this picture in important ways.

First, it has been pointed out that fascism was not essentially un-British. The intellectual origins of fascist ideology were certainly not alien to Britain. The racialist component in fascism was a commonplace to many Britons. It was a Briton, Houston Stewart Chamberlain, who developed the idea that the Teutonic race was a master race and that the Jews were inferior. Anti-Semitism was very common in Britain before, during and after the First World War, and the British empire was based on crude racial assumptions. In 1936 the fascist newspaper *Blackshirt* insisted that 'the people of Britain are temperamentally and spiritually fitted to assume the leadership of the nations of the earth', an idea British imperialists had been supporting for decades. Nor was everyone in Britain committed to democracy. There were a number of people dismayed at the arrival of universal suffrage and who preferred the sort of paternal rule which went on in the colonies. The fascist idea that life is a struggle in which only the fittest survive also had British origins, deriving from the evolutionary theories of Charles Darwin. It was the British philosopher Herbert Spencer who coined the phrase 'the survival of the fittest'. Nor should we imagine that the BUF was the first fascist group to be formed in Britain. Mosley's organisation was set up after 'The Britons', 'The British Fascists' (two of whose members won council seats in 1924), the 'Fascist League' and the 'Imperial Fascist League'. Similarly the BUF was not the last such body, being followed after the Second World War by the 'National Front' and other groups. There were, admittedly, fewer traditions of militarism than on the continent, but it was certainly not inevitable that fascism would fail in Britain.

Nor is it fair to dismiss Mosley himself as a playboy. He certainly lacked political stability in his early years. He was a Conservative in the early-1920s and joined Labour in 1926, even serving as a minister in the second Labour government, before setting up the New Party in 1931. The following year, after a visit to Rome in which he was able to observe, and admire, the fascist dictator Benito Mussolini, he began the BUF, dressing his supporters in the black shirts sported by the Italians. Yet from that moment on, his commitment to fascism was long-lasting. Despite a reputation for sexual immorality (which, it has been said, 'made Lloyd George look like a virgin') he was also dedicated and hard-working. It has been calculated that in his first five years as a fascist he made over 100 speeches a year, as well as writing three books – one of which, *Greater Britain*, is said to be far and away intellectually superior to Hitler's *Mein Kampf* – and a hundred articles. Nor was his ability insubstantial. As an orator, he would

Similar to Churchill in this respect

usually speak for an hour and a half without notes. One journalist described him as 'the sort of orator who could thrill a multitude by declaiming the explanatory notes on an income-tax form'. He also had the ability to win devoted supporters, one of whom insisted that

THE BUILDERS

Signor Mussolini: 'I have arranged for a new Rome to arise within five years.'

John Bull (aside): 'And to think that London's taken nearly twice that time to decide about keeping one bridge where it was.'

[Like the Soviet Government, Signor Mussolini has a Five Years Plan. It includes not only the rebuilding of Rome, but its junction with the sea by a canal and the construction of a vast harbour, to be named Port Mussolini, in the neighbourhood of the new city.]

Cartoon from *Punch*, *1932*.

Mosley was 'a giant in a pygmy world. A man among men. Oswald Mosley would leave Christ standing at first base.'

Mosley's memorandum on unemployment, submitted to the Labour cabinet in 1930 (see page 73), had already marked him down as a constructive economic thinker. By 1931, as the depression deepened, he came to the conclusion that parliamentary democracy could not possibly solve the country's problems. Mosley, like many others, believed that while British politicians debated and dithered, the fascist leader Mussolini was reviving Italian glory and achieving bold and substantial reform (see the *Punch* cartoon on page 123). He insisted in 1932 that Britain's system was a hundred years out of date – it was the system of 1832. The idea that voters should elect a government to do a job and also elect an opposition to stop them doing it would, Mosley insisted, be regarded in the light of history as 'a curious and temporary aberration of the human mind'. He believed that key economic decisions should be taken by technical experts not oratorical windbags. He would allow an elected parliament to exist and to vote, but legislation would be the preserve of a five-man cabinet under a powerful prime minister (himself). His programme was a strange combination of Italian fascism and Keynesian economics. He was also influenced by a faith in science and mass production, derived from a visit to the United States, and by a vision of developing the British empire into a self-contained economic unit. His experiences in the trenches in the First World War were also of great importance for his thought: the senseless slaughter on the western front led him to believe that human beings needed a new radical commitment to restore meaning to otherwise purposeless lives. Whether in fact Mosley was an important political thinker is an issue which is hotly contested amongst historians.

b) The Rise of the BUF

Mosley achieved marked initial success, and the BUF soon found important sponsors. In particular Lord Rothermere, owner of the *Daily Mail*, lent his support; an article on the British fascists in the *Mail* bore the headline 'Hurrah for the Blackshirts!', and enrolment forms were actually printed in the paper. By April 1934 the BUF had 50,000 members (far more than was once believed), and the future looked bright for British fascism. A rally at the Albert Hall in this month was a great success, and another was to be held at Olympia (with a seating capacity of 13,000) in June. In fact the Olympia meeting was a turning point in Mosley's fortunes. Violent scuffles broke out at the meeting and over 50 hecklers were roughly ejected by fascist stewards, of whom there were about 1,000 present.

Police were not allowed into Olympia – they could only enter such a private meeting if they saw a breach of the peace taking place – but officers were stationed outside. A constable commented on the scene:

1 At intervals the door was flung open and one or more persons ejected
into the main road. In nearly every case they were bleeding from the
head and face and their clothing was badly torn ... The situation was at
periods a little ugly but in almost all these cases it was through the
5 action of the stewards.

A police inspector did enter the building when he saw an injured man
lying near the entrance:

1 On looking down the hall I saw six groups, each containing six to eight
Blackshirts beating and kicking unmercifully a man in the centre of each
group. In three instances the men assaulted were lying on the ground
... When we had succeeded in rescuing all we could see, agonising cries
5 came from the foot of the stairs and there we found four Blackshirts
with a weak youth on his back on the stairs. He was being beaten in a
brutal manner. When we rescued him he was scarcely able to walk.

Yet when asked by his superiors why he had not arrested the
Blackshirts, the inspector replied that perhaps, after all, he had not
seen them actually beating their victims!

A journalist from the *Sunday Dispatch* also described, in his diary,
what he saw at Olympia:

1 The first interrupter raised his voice to shout some interjection. The
mob of storm troops hurled itself at him. He was battered and biffed
and bashed and dragged out – while the tentative sympathisers all about
him ... grew sick and began to think of escape. From that moment it
5 was a shambles. Free fights all over the show. The Fascist technique is
really the most brutal thing I have ever seen, which is saying something.
There is no pause to hear what the interrupter is saying: there is no tap
on the shoulder and a request to leave quietly: there is only the mass
assault. Once a man's arms are pinioned, his face is common property
10 to all adjacent punchers ... We left at about 10.30, with Mosley still
speaking.

In his memoirs Mosley defended the actions of his stewards and put
the blame on the hecklers:

1 A collection of weapons taken from the attackers was afterwards made
and the photographs are still on record. Our stewards had to eject
these armed men with their bare hands, for they were not only forbid-
den to carry weapons, but they were often searched to ensure the
5 order was obeyed. Our Constitution laid down precise rules for dealing with disorders at meetings: 'Interrupters will be ejected only on the
instructions of the speaker as chairman of the meeting when the per-
sistence of an interrupter prevents those in his vicinity from hearing the
speech. Ejection will be carried out with the minimum of force necess-
10 ary to secure the removal of the interrupter from the meeting.' Were
our stewards really to be blamed if they punched with their fists men
who attacked them with 'razors, knuckle-dusters and iron bars' [as a

Conservative MP testified]? If they handled the opposition with such brutality, why was not a single case of that kind detained in London hos-
15 pitals that night? At our own dressing-station, according to signed statements of highly qualified medical personnel: 'Sixty-three Blackshirts were treated for injuries, mostly abdominal, mostly caused by blunt instruments' ... Why then did we find it necessary to organise a dressing-station at Olympia, which we intended to be another political meet-
20 ing to convert the British people to our cause? ... The answer is that the attack on the meeting was openly organised in advance. We knew all about it ...

c) The Decline of the BUF

Mosley had probably not wished to use violent tactics. At Olympia he had wanted to be heard, but communists and Jews disrupted the meeting. One communist heckler, Joe Jacobs, has recalled that 'So effective was our penetration into Olympia that despite repeated attempts, Mosley was unable to make his speech heard because of the noise and fighting between his stewards and supporters and the anti-fascists.' A distinction ought perhaps to be made in 1932–4 between Mosley and some of his lieutenants: many of the latter were far more anti-Semitic than their leader and favoured violence much more than he did. At all events, the media tended to blame the BUF for the violence at Olympia and depicted Mosley's stewards as Nazi stormtroopers. Rothermere hastily distanced himself from Mosley. One year later membership had declined to a mere 5,000.

Mosley was in a difficult position. He had imagined that the depression would get worse and that – somehow or other – he would emerge as Britain's saviour. But, for the majority of British workers, economic conditions began to improve. In addition, the BUF had lost its respectability because of a reputation for violence and was being damned by association with events on the continent – especially in Germany, where Hitler was becoming more anti-Semitic, more aggressive in his foreign policy and more violent against his enemies, as in the 'Night of the Long Knives' at the end of June 1934, when around 100 rivals were killed. But by 1935–6, partly as a reaction to the tactics of the communist opposition, Mosley had become more openly anti-Semitic and more clearly identified with Nazism. Above his desk, he had photographs of George V, Mussolini and Hitler. In 1936 he changed the title of his party to the 'British Union of Fascists and National Socialists', and in the same year he married, in Berlin, a woman, Diana Mitford, who idolised Hitler.

d) The Recovery and Fall of the BUF

This change of tactics halted the decline of the Fascist Union. There was a smaller membership than in 1934 but it was a more committed one. Mosley found it harder to hire halls after the Olympia experience, so he organised marches in the streets instead, especially in the east end of London (in order to bait the Jewish householders, said his critics, though Mosley said it was because his strongest support was in this area). As his biographer, Robert Skidelsky, has written, Mosley may not have gone looking for fights, but 'avoiding them was not his chief priority'. One such march, soon to be known as the Battle of Cable Street, was held in October 1936. Fascists gathered at the Royal Mint and headed towards the east end, but they were met by around 100,000 anti-fascists who erected barricades in Cable Street. The police were unable to clear a way. In the ensuing fighting well over 100 people were injured and about 100 were arrested. This incident seemed further evidence that the BUF produced violence, and the government decided to take action. In 1934 the Incitement to Disaffection Act had extended police powers to search for seditious literature, but had been little used. Now the Public Order Act of 1936 banned the wearing of political uniforms and gave the police new powers to ban meetings and processions. Many historians have claimed that this low-key response to British fascism was a wise reaction. Certainly it was a real blow to the blackshirts, who were not allowed to wear even an arm-band to distinguish themselves from the general public. Yet in fact fascism did not decline. In December 1936 when the act was passed the BUF had around 15,000 members, but by 1939 there were over 22,000.

The movement enjoyed most support in the north of England, and Mosley even contemplated transferring his headquarters from London to Manchester. While not contesting the 1935 general election, Mosley decided that he would fight the next one and by 1939 had chosen 80 candidates. Fascists did stand in municipal elections in the east end of London in February 1937, winning 18 per cent of the vote. But above all Mosley relied on rallies on particular political topics. In 1936 he tried to rouse support in a 'Stand by the King' campaign, protesting against the forced abdication of Edward VIII. His best card was a series of campaigns built around the slogan 'Mind Britain's Business'. It was probably this issue which was responsible for the growth of fascist support by 1939. Mosley insisted that events on the continent were none of Britain's business and that Hitler should be given a free hand in eastern Europe. He built on isolationist sentiment in Britain, and at the same time insisted that, as a true patriot, he would fight to the death against anyone who threatened Britain's real interests. Yet this issue also revealed the fundamental weaknesses of British fascism. No one could argue that Chamberlain, with his policy of appeasement, was rushing headlong into war. The British government was giving Hitler every chance to accept a peaceful solution to Germany's legitimate grievances, and as the 1930s proceeded it became more and more obvious that Nazi aggression was a menace to the peace of Europe. In the public eye, therefore, the British fascists were a potentially dangerous fifth column: to be a British fascist was to appear inherently disloyal. Certainly when the war did break out, on 3 September 1939, support for the BUF collapsed. Mosley and other leading fascists were interned in 1940. Public criticism of government action towards the fascists only began in 1943, when Mosley, who had lost over three stones in weight, was released because of poor health.

e) Why did the BUF fail?

Fascism undoubtedly failed in Britain, and there are more than enough reasons to explain its failure. Contemporaries pointed out that Britain had two significant 'safety valves' not available to countries like Germany. First, people's 'leader worship' was directed not towards politicians, who might be corrupted by adulation, but towards the politically impotent monarchy; and, secondly, those with fascist or sadistic impulses had been drawn away from Britain itself towards the British empire, where they could govern the so-called 'lesser breeds without the law'. Yet today these seem minor factors. Nor do modern historians see government legislation as crucial in fascist failure, though the banning of political uniforms was a wise move. Nor can we be so certain that Mosley himself lacked constructive abilities, though his leading lieutenants, several of whom were obsessed with anti-Semitism, may well have been liabilities. But Mosley certainly never worked out any method for achieving power – he was an opportunist for whom no opportunity ever arose – and nor did he attract the financial support which the party needed. His supporters too seem to have been lacking in real calibre, being 'marginal' men and women. One BUF supporter, a women's district leader in Lancashire, has commented that 'For every good normal member, we got several who were cranks – and worse ... with waste paper basket ideas ... It was almost like a comic opera.'

The circumstances in which Mosley operated were undoubtedly inauspicious. In 1932 he assumed that the future lay with fascism; but in fact, as we can now see, the various movements in Europe which have been called fascist had little in common with each other. Even Mussolini and Hitler had noticeable points of difference. In short, although democracy was being eclipsed on the continent, there was no fascist bandwagon in Europe likely to draw its supporters into power. Mosley had fundamentally misunderstood the nature of the European crisis. Furthermore the economic depression began to ease almost as soon as the BUF had been formed, and Britain's parliamentary institutions proved remarkably resilient, much more so than in Italy or Germany. Nor was there in Britain a highly visible communist threat. At no time did a communist revolution seem a possibility and so the fascists could not benefit from such fears. The polarisation which occurred in Germany in the early-1930s between extreme left and extreme right did not happen in Britain. On the other hand, the communists did much to counterattack the extreme right and to tear away the veil of respectability that the BUF initially wore. Finally patriotism – a force Mosley had hoped to make his own – spelt final defeat for fascism as Britain approached and joined the Second World War. By September 1939 the British were united against Hitler and there was no room for the extreme right on the political scene. Fascism had become un-British.

5 Conclusion

> **KEY ISSUE** How significant were the extremist groups in the 1930s?

The 1930s did see important political changes in Britain. The Labour party was, in effect, preparing itself for government – for what turned out to be an important role in the war-time coalition and a majority administration after the war. At the extremes of politics, the communists and the fascists made the 1930s a period of intense ideological conflict and a decade of unaccustomed political agitation on the streets. It has been argued that extra-parliamentary political activity in Britain in the late-1930s reached new heights, and, according to one writer, there were more widespread 'mass movements' in Britain in 1936–8 than at any time since Chartism in the mid-nineteenth century. More research is needed on these years, but it is probably true to say that while Communist Party and BUF membership can be measured in tens of thousands, millions of people participated in some way in new forms of political activity – whether in demonstrations, in making donations or in reading the relevant literature. Rank and file trade unionists were much more sympathetic to left-wing causes than their official leaders. Certainly the police were unusually active in the 1930s and sometimes used baton-charges quite ruthlessly.

The extremist parties of the 1930s are well worth studying, for they constitute an important aspect of political life in the decade. However, they must be seen in perspective. The great majority of British people never thought of joining them and, when they were given the chance, did not vote for them. Fascists and communists add to our understanding of the interwar period, but mostly by throwing into relief the achievements of the democratic parties, which survived the depression intact. There was volatility in the 1930s, but what really stands out is the degree of stability and, some would say, political apathy.

In the 1930s the extreme left and the extreme right balanced each other; they had about the same number of supporters and therefore each neutralised the other. They were almost mirror images of each other, though at opposite ends of the political spectrum: both authoritarian, both failing in elections, both taking to the streets, and both damned in the public mind by being associated with foreign powers. Indeed they needed each other – though no one ever admitted it – for the one provided the *raison d'être* for the other, and neither could afford to win total victory. While this elaborate charade was being played out, politicians got on with the business of governing Britain.

Summary Diagram
Opposition in the 1930s

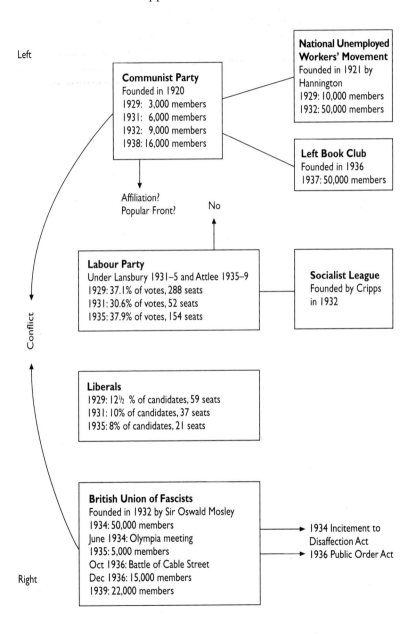

Left

National Unemployed Workers' Movement
Founded in 1921 by Hannington
1929: 10,000 members
1932: 50,000 members

Communist Party
Founded in 1920
1929: 3,000 members
1931: 6,000 members
1932: 9,000 members
1938: 16,000 members

Left Book Club
Founded in 1936
1937: 50,000 members

Affiliation?
Popular Front?

No

Labour Party
Under Lansbury 1931–5 and Attlee 1935–9
1929: 37.1% of votes, 288 seats
1931: 30.6% of votes, 52 seats
1935: 37.9% of votes, 154 seats

Socialist League
Founded by Cripps in 1932

Conflict

Liberals
1929: 12½ % of candidates, 59 seats
1931: 10% of candidates, 37 seats
1935: 8% of candidates, 21 seats

British Union of Fascists
Founded in 1932 by Sir Oswald Mosley
1934: 50,000 members
June 1934: Olympia meeting
1935: 5,000 members
Oct 1936: Battle of Cable Street
Dec 1936: 15,000 members
1939: 22,000 members

1934 Incitement to Disaffection Act
1936 Public Order Act

Right

Working on Chapter 6

Try to organise your notes around a) the ideas or policies of a particular group and b) the actions or events with which they were concerned. Make particularly detailed notes on Mosley and the BUF. Try to put the reasons for fascist failure in Britain into some sort of order of importance.

Answering essay questions on Chapter 6

Since the mid-1970s a great deal has been written on British fascism, and questions on this topic are becoming increasingly common. A typical example is:

1. Account for the failure of fascism to win mass support in Britain in the 1930s.

Construct an essay plan for this question by writing your own 'structured question'. Which sub-divisions will you choose? Useful ones might be 'What level of support did the BUF achieve after 1932?', 'Did Mosley prove an able leader?' and 'Were economic conditions conducive to the growth of the BUF?' But there are many more. A good answer will require you to utilise your knowledge of the extreme left in the same period. A few references to fascism in Europe would also impress the examiners.

Source-based questions on Chapter 6

1. Contrasting views on the Olympia meeting
Read the extracts on pages 125 and 126 and answer the following questions:

a) How conclusive do you find the evidence of the police constable and the police inspector? Explain your answer. (*6 marks*)
b) Might the journalist be thought guilty of naïvete and of being contraddictory? Explain your answer. (*5 marks*)
c) In what ways is the extract from Mosley's memoirs inconsistent with the evidence in the other sources? (*6 marks*)
d) What do you think is the significance of Mosley's statement that the blackshirts knew all about anti-fascist plans to infiltrate the Olympia meeting? (*3 marks*)
d) How far is it possible, on the basis of these extracts and of other knowledge you have, to reach firm conclusions about the responsibility for the violence at Olympia? Explain you answer. (*10 marks*)

7 The Interwar Years: a Conclusion

POINTS TO CONSIDER

This chapter seeks to consider the interwar years as a whole and to decide what judgements we may legitimately make. But rather than telling you what to think, it urges you to formulate your own verdict.

1 A Basis for Judgement

KEY ISSUE Why is it so difficult to formulate historical judgements?

'The conclusion is that there is no conclusion.' Anyone completing a volume on the political history of Britain between the wars is likely to be tempted to end with some such phrase. There is of course justification for this view, given that there can be no conclusion in the sense of 'final verdict' on this or indeed any other period of the past. History never allows that degree of certainty. But historians should at least try to make provisional judgements, and be willing to change them in the light of further evidence. We should lift our eyes from the precise details – from the events and individuals, and from the memoranda and speeches and other evidence – and consider the 1918–39 period as a whole. Detailed research gives us knowledge about the past, but only by attempting to see the connections between events and formulate overall judgements can we come close to real understanding of it.

This final chapter must therefore do more than summarise the previous ones. We must attempt to formulate reasonable and rational provisional judgements on the politics of Britain from 1918 to 1939. Yet even this is an immensely difficult task and, paradoxically, the best students of history will probably be the ones least satisfied with their efforts.

What are the problems involved? To begin with, there is the danger of over-generalising. We must generalise if we are to make sense of the complexity of the past and yet because history is so complex it is difficult to generalise without distorting. Inadequate generalisations reduce rather than enhance our historical understanding. There is also the issue of which areas of the past we select for scrutiny. The interwar period comprises only 21 years, and yet the evidence that survives is almost mountainous. The activities of politicians were so varied that we have to choose which areas to study and highlight, or we get nowhere. So how do we make our selection? Clearly we cannot seize on single events or individuals: we must look instead at broad categories. The following list is to some extent arbitrary, but at least it provides a starting point:

1. Economic affairs.
2. Foreign policy.
3. Social reforms.
4. Politics at Westminster: politicians and political parties.
5. The growth and survival of democracy.

These topics seem to cover most of the important issues of the 1920s and 1930s, but it is worthwhile thinking about what other broad categories or headings might be included.

An attempt must be made to examine each of these broad areas in the interwar period and to reach sensible judgements based squarely on our knowledge of what occurred. Of course, we all try to be 'sensible' and some people believe that common sense is the most important tool the historian needs. But the formulation of judgements is in fact a very complicated process, and students should appreciate some of the stages and the issues involved in it. Certainly we should all be aware of the criteria (or yardsticks) by which we make our assessments.

The main conventional judgement historians use is 'success' or 'failure'. But not all historians state explicitly how they distinguish the one from the other. There are two main schools of thought. The first stresses the criterion of people's aims and whether they achieved their aims. This, essentially, involves judging people by the standards of their times and avoiding the use of hindsight. The other, on the contrary, uses hindsight to highlight the long(er)-term effects of actions. By this criterion, an action may be judged a success even though, at the time it took place, it may have seemed a failure, and *vice versa*. Historians often write of the 'historical significance' of an event, by which they usually mean what it led on to and how it connected with later events. In this light, the original aims of those responsible for an action may be quite irrelevant to its significance and its success.

Another common criterion involves assessing an achievement alongside what could or should have been done. We often read, for instance, that a certain reform, which in itself might seem impressive, was very unimpressive when compared with the opportunities that existed, and so much so that 'success' must in fact be adjudged 'failure'. (The opposite is, of course, also the case: achievements may seem all the more remarkable in view of the problems to be overcome and the likelihood of failure.) Those who employ this criterion imply not simply that errors were made, but that preventable errors were committed. Such judgements may well be valid; but the problem with this method is that we can never quite be certain what could have been done or would have been achieved if people had acted differently. The issue of 'what would have happened' – the hypothetical – is slippery ground.

A similar criterion also involves comparison. The achievements of a particular period are often compared with those of another period of the same country or with the same period in a different country. Such a comparison gives us grounds for making relative judgements, and yet of course this too is a method which must be used with caution, since circumstances vary from place to place and from time to time, and so we are not always comparing like with like.

A great deal depends on the criteria one uses and, above all, on the angle of vision – the perspective – from which we view past events. Should we try to use the angle of vision, and the values, of the interwar years themselves and attempt to exclude our own values? Or should we judge from a present-day vantage point and make use of hindsight? Some historians try to see events from the points of view of the people involved in them. This view 'from the inside' (the attempt to empathise with the people of the past) tends to produce sympathetic judgements. Others try to distance themselves and sometimes to act as judges, praising and, much more often for the interwar years, condemning. Most historians probably try to do both, attempting to see events from the perspective of historical figures themselves and also to trace the longer-term consequences of their actions.

Clearly there is no particular set of criteria which all historians use. This is a reflection of the fact that historical judgements can never be totally objective. All judgements tell us not only about the object or event under scrutiny, but about the biases and values of the observer. The historian is part of the process of history, not a god able to judge objectively from above. It is important to remember this, especially for recent history which still arouses political passions. Many of the most important historians of the interwar years were alive between the wars and felt emotionally as well as intellectually involved with its issues. The rest of us have political views, which often 'colour' our interpretations of political history.

Enough has been said to indicate what a complex business the formulation of historical judgements is! Nevertheless the attempt to formulate provisional historical judgements is a vital part of studying history, and one of the most exciting and rewarding. The more conscious we are of the methods we use and of the criteria we employ in formulating our verdicts, the more reasonable and acceptable our conclusions are likely to be.

2 'Rule by Pygmies'

> **KEY ISSUE** In what ways was 1918–39 a period of abject failure?

By the 1960s a broad consensus had emerged about the interwar years. It was portrayed as a time of mediocrity and failure – a period of 'rule by pygmies', in Mowat's phrase – between more successful and glamorous eras. 1918–39 was sandwiched between two world wars, in both of which Britain fought successfully to decide the future of Europe and of the world. In comparison, the years after the First World War seem petty and unsuccessful. The opportunities presented by the peace in 1918 were squandered, so that another world war started in 1939. Politicians in other periods did much better. Before 1914 the Liberal government of Asquith was a reforming administration which laid the foundations for the welfare state. After 1945 Attlee's Labour government set up the National Health Service, completed the welfare state and established the 'mixed economy' by nationalising important sectors of British industry. In contrast, the interwar years seem uninspiring and relatively unimportant. 1918–39 were simply 'the years in between'.

According to this interpretation, interwar politicians were unadventurous and rather timid men who achieved very little. They failed in all the important areas, both foreign and domestic. In foreign policy they failed to stand up to German aggression. Britain was much stronger than Germany in the key years that followed Hitler's rise to power, and its leaders should have resolutely opposed the Nazi dictator; but instead they pandered to him and increased his appetite for territory. Appeasement was thus a foolish and cowardly policy and the Second World War was the 'unnecessary war' that resulted from it. Similarly Britain's leaders failed to formulate an effective economic strategy, placidly accepting an horrific level of mass unemployment, even though Keynes had formulated a viable strategy that would have cured the problem. Churchill described Britain's leaders in the 1930s as 'decided only to be undecided, adamant for drift, solid for fluidity, all powerful to be impotent'. Not surprisingly, such men had no real answer to poor industrial relations (other than to allow strikes to take their course), while their record of social reform was low-key and unimaginative. Thus the period is typified by failures and missed opportunities.

Small wonder, according to Mowat and others, that many young British intellectuals came to the conclusion that Britain was decadent and that the future lay with Soviet communism. It was a period of despair. Only in the Second World War did Britain 'find itself' again and shake itself free from the lethargy and aimless mediocrity of the interwar years.

This interpretation has the advantages of clarity and forcefulness. It also sees the interwar period very much as a unity. As a unifying cause, over and above the weak-kneed politicians, it points to the First World War. The war produced a mood of. introspection. The intellectuals, partly as a result of the slaughter on the western front, lost their belief in progress, their confidence that things would, almost automatically, get better and better. Much of the literature of the years 1918 to 1939 is pessimistic and depressing, and many of its leading intellectual figures were prophets of doom. (T.S. Eliot, for instance, referred to the years '*l'entre deux guerres*' as 'twenty years largely wasted'.) Clearly the British had lost confidence in themselves. A whole generation did not perish in the war, but significant numbers did, and as a result there was a shortage of new blood in politics. After 1918 the leading figures were old men: Asquith was 74 when he gave up the leadership of the Liberal party, and Lloyd George was 68 when he resigned the same position; MacDonald was 69 when he stood down as prime minister, giving way to Baldwin, who handed over at the age of 70 to the 68-year old Neville Chamberlain. There was also great continuity of personnel in the Commons when, arguably, an infusion of new talent was needed. Half of the MPs of 1914 were still sitting in the House in 1939.

3 A Critique of the Traditional Interpretation

> **KEY ISSUE** Why do the ultra-critical interpretations of earlier decades now seem inadequate?

The idea of 'the years in between' is no longer acceptable to many historians. It seems to them to beg serious questions. Were the world wars really eras of triumph and fulfilment for Britain, and were the Asquith and Attlee administrations as uniformly successful as they have often been described? In addition, the traditional interpretation is simplistic in that it does not allow for the great variety that existed between 1918 and 1939. In particular, an excessive concentration on the economic problems of the time is likely to be viewed by these historians as 'distorting' rather than 'generalising', for not all of industry was depressed. Nor does the traditional view take enough account of the 'standards of the time'. If, for instance, the 1931–5 government was such an abysmal failure, why did electors at the general election of 1935 re-elect it for a second term of office? Mowat and other historians writing in the 1950s and 1960s seem to have employed hindsight to give a very unbalanced account.

The critics of the interwar period have used as one of their major criteria the hypothetical idea of what could or should have been done. In other words, they believe that Britain's politicians wasted opportunities and that greater success was open to them. But such a view now seems to tell us as much, if not more, about the time in which it was formulated as about the interwar years. There was great confidence in the 1950s and early 1960s that governments could maintain high levels of employment by using Keynesian techniques and, basically, spend their way out of recessions – and therefore the economic record between the wars looked especially poor. Interwar politicians seemed to have ignored simple solutions to their economic problems. Similarly, historians after the Second World War accepted the version of British foreign policy that Winston Churchill, the arch anti-appeaser, had made popular. This was the view that appeasement was wilfully blind and that the war could have been avoided if Britain had stood up to Hitler earlier. But today neither of these two charges is generally accepted. There now seems no simple way out of an economic depression – especially after our experiences of inflation and unemployment in the 1970s, 1980s and early 1990s. Keynesian policies have been tried and, most experts agree, found wanting. Also, our fuller appreciation of Britain's vulnerable and over-stretched international position in the 1930s makes appeasement seem a natural policy for Britain to have followed.

These two issues – mass unemployment and appeasement – are still crucial and controversial issues, but the opening of government archives under the 30-year rule has enabled us to see politicians' problems from the perspective of the policy-makers themselves. No longer do historians tend to be as harsh in their judgements as Mowat and his contemporaries were. Greater distance from the 1930s also makes historians more dispassionate and less concerned to pass moral judgements on the politicians of the time. In addition, rather than comparing the interwar period with Britain before and after, to the detriment of 1918–39, it is becoming more common to compare Britain in the 1920s and 1930s with other countries in those decades. Such a comparison highlights an issue which Mowat and others tended to take for granted – the survival and growth of democracy in Britain.

4 A Review of the Key Areas

> **KEY ISSUE** What provisional judgements should we make on the politicians' record?

Historians can never be totally objective, and indeed the two main schools of thought on the interwar period depend to some degree upon the outlooks of the historians involved. These schools might be best described as the 'pessimists' and the 'optimists'. A review of their interpretations will, it is hoped, encourage readers to make up their own minds and to formulate their own judgements about the period as a whole. Of course, doing so may initially provoke some confusion – but then confusion forces us to think hard and is probably a necessary stage in the development of clarity. All students of history should decide for themselves what provisional judgements are acceptable on each topic they study. They should also be aware of the criteria for judgement that they are employing.

a) The Economy

The interwar years were marked by high unemployment which was centred in certain depressed areas. These were those parts of the country which had spearheaded the creation of British wealth in the nineteenth century but whose products were not needed in such quantities after the First World War. For them the interwar years were therefore a painful period of economic readjustment. It has been argued that mass unemployment and under-utilised capacity justify 'a pessimistic conclusion on the economic achievements of interwar Britain'. But in some areas of the country, where the new consumer goods industries were located, this readjustment was successful and produced much prosperity. On average, wages increased in real terms (that is, in relation to prices) by one-third between 1913 and 1938. Perhaps therefore the 1930s should be seen as the forerunner not of the austerity of 1940–50 but of the affluence of the 1950s. Which view should we accept? Should we come down on the side of either depression or prosperity? (Perhaps the first view is that of someone towards the left of the political spectrum – a believer in state intervention – whereas the second may be the view of someone to the right, who believes in 'market forces' and wants to see a return to the *laissez-faire* that existed before the Second World War.) To talk of the 'Hungry Thirties', as though all Britons throughout the decade were uniformly afflicted with poverty, may be quite as misleading as to speak of the 'Affluent Thirties'. Both may be no more than half-truths – and it takes two halves to make a whole.

What credit or blame should governments take for Britain's economic performance? It is perfectly reasonable to reach either 'harsh' or 'sympathetic' judgements. Mistakes certainly were made, as with the return to the gold standard at the pre-war parity in 1925, and almost all politicians showed a lack of real economic expertise. They tended to be rather timid and unwilling ever to experiment. They were possibly encouraged in this by the fact that the unemployed were confined to a relatively small number of (Labour) constituencies, instead of being spread evenly throughout the electorate. This meant that the outcome of a general election was unlikely to hinge on the issue of unemployment. Yet it should be recognised that politicians in this period did not possess the statistical evidence about the economy which is a necessary pre-condition for effective action. Nor was there any generally agreed solution to which they could turn. Keynes's ideas were not fully worked out, and nor should it be assumed that they would have worked. In a society that does not have a centrally controlled economy, any policy that is to be successful must take account of business confidence, and Keynes's ideas were regarded with a deep-rooted suspicion by most industrialists. John Ramsden has even argued that, in the circumstances of 1931, a

Keynesian policy 'might well have led to financial collapse, not because it was wrong but because it was believed to be wrong'.

Our view of the refusal of politicians to adopt Keynesian techniques is often greatly influenced by hindsight, and especially by Britain's economic performance since 1945. However, it is as well to consider the aims of the policy-makers themselves. They consciously opted for a strategy of 'safety first' and put their emphasis on the avoidance of economic collapse. Using this criterion, they did reasonably well. Maybe there was no economic renaissance, but there was no economic catastrophe either. None of the democracies coped noticeably better with the great depression than Britain, not even the United States, where mass unemployment still existed in the late-1930s. Yet, rather than praise or condemn the politicians, we may be tempted to agree with the cynic who wrote that 'when the economy is going right, the politicians can do nothing wrong; and when the economy is going wrong, the politicians can do nothing right.'

b) Foreign policy

British foreign policy 1918–39 has also been the subject of much controversy, stemming in part from the different criteria that historians have employed. In retrospect, it is easy to see the flaws of the Versailles peace treaty. Germany was neither crushed nor conciliated: instead she was given a sense of grievance and left with the basic resources to become dominant in Europe. Hindsight allows us to trace the origins of the Second World War back to Versailles. Yet in view of the circumstances of 1918, when feelings against Germany were running so high that debates were held in the British press over whether the Kaiser should be boiled in oil or merely hung, drawn and quartered, the settlement was certainly understandable. For the rest of the 1920s British policy-makers sincerely attempted to achieve pacification in Europe and to promote friendship between France and Germany. Later events showed that there was a good measure of delusion in the 'Locarno years', but at least the leading nations were talking to each other and were reaching a substantial measure of agreement. In the following decade Hitler's actions shattered the peace. Britain's policy of appeasement will long be debated. Historians have generally been too ready to take up extreme positions on this subject. Appeasement was not a clear-sighted, dynamic policy: it had elements of muddled and wishful thinking in it. Yet it is by no means certain that a more forceful British stance would have deterred Hitler, even if it had proved acceptable to British public opinion and the House of Commons, and at least appeasement was based upon an accurate assessment of Britain's economic decline and upon an appreciation of the British empire's vulnerability to the Japanese and Italians, as well as the Germans. At all events, Chamberlain was able to take Britain into war in September 1939 as a united nation – much more united than it had been in 1914.

The extent to which Britain was responsible for the Second World War is an issue everyone should think about. If the war was preventable, perhaps those who failed to prevent it should take a share of the blame. However, many historians have insisted that British politicians should be praised for labouring for harmony in European affairs and that, although they failed, the blame for another world war must be put squarely on the aggressors and not the peacemakers.

c) Social Reforms

The 1918–39 period cannot be seen as one of spectacular social reform. The high hopes of 1918–20, that Britain could be transformed into a 'land fit for heroes', were quickly dashed. There were far more legislative achievements in 1906–14 and 1945–51. Yet if we compare Britain's social reforms with those, say, in France or Italy, then Britain's record does not seem as bleak as it has traditionally been portrayed. After all, reforms of significance were introduced. There were reforms in housing, in extending unemployment benefit and providing 'uncovenanted benefit' (the dole), in establishing a proper system of old age and widows' pensions, in improving the supply of electricity and in reorganising local government. Do these reforms support the idea that politicians were simply 'marking time'? Even the first Labour government, which aimed merely to gain experience of the system, came up with Wheatley's Housing Act. And though there were significant differences in health standards between the social classes, average life expectancy did grow in the interwar period by six years.

To later generations, with different standards and higher expectations, this social legislation may seem somewhat disappointing. Perhaps much more could and should have been done. Some have judged that politicians were more concerned with winning and keeping power at Westminster than with solving the country's social and economic problems. Yet the 'defenders' have insisted that, although British governments between the wars were certainly not radical, even Conservative governments were not conservative – that is, they did not favour the *status quo*. Instead, they fostered moderately progressive changes. The 'diehard' wing of the Conservative party did not generally get its way. No doubt more might have been achieved had the political will existed, but even so by 1939 British social services – however inadequate they seem by later standards – were among the most comprehensive in the world. Perhaps the real weakness between the wars was, in sharp contrast to the dictatorships, a lack of effective propaganda proclaiming British achievements.

d) Politicians and Political Parties

When we consider the politicians of the interwar period we immediately think of Baldwin and MacDonald, the two prime ministers who held power for longest. Both have attracted contrasting judgements. They certainly had their failings, and in particular they were not bold and original thinkers or legislators. Critical historians, applying the criterion of what they could or should have done, have dismissed them as pygmies and second-rate figures. Yet if we use the criteria of 'the standards of the time' and whether they achieved their aims, we can see that they had their strengths and successes. They were determined to preserve democracy and to achieve a political consensus that would diminish rather than sharpen class differences, and in this they were largely successful. Admittedly they lacked the dynamism and talent of Lloyd George, but they were also remarkably free of his faults, and were certainly more in tune with public opinion. Their enormous electoral popularity should not be forgotten. Baldwin and MacDonald were in some ways undynamic and unheroic figures, but perhaps this was appropriate in what was really an unheroic age. They may have been poor at leading or forming public opinion, but they were excellent at reflecting it. For good or ill, Britain had become a democracy, and the will of the electorate ruled. The novelist George Orwell, an outspoken critic who judged that the public was fed on an unwholesome political diet of 'sugar and water' between the wars, conceded that it was 'almost certain that between 1931 and 1940 the National Government represented the will of the mass of the people'. Perhaps Britain got the politicians it deserved.

The debate about the political stature and calibre of Baldwin and MacDonald (and other figures like Lloyd George, Bonar Law, Henderson and the Chamberlains), and their place in British history, continues and no final verdict is possible. All that is claimed here is that they were highly complex historical figures, well worthy of study – as worthy as the politicians of earlier and later periods.

The interwar years were indeed rich in political diversity and controversy. The decline of the Liberal party and the rise of Labour were political trends of immense significance, as was the consolidation of Conservative power. Indeed the pre-eminence of Baldwin and MacDonald owed much to the party system in Britain, which rested on the 'first past the post system' which traditionally gave an overall majority to the strongest party, even though it usually lacked a majority of popular votes. It is a system that can be praised or criticised. It certainly did not produce as representative a parliament as those seen in France or in Germany (before 1933), where forms of proportional representation were employed and where dozens of parties existed. But, on the other hand, it did make for stability in terms of governments. Few historians have argued that this trade-off was unacceptable, especially in view of the collapse of the democratic Weimar Republic in Germany and the inadequacies of the Third French Republic.

The British party system had its drawbacks. In 1929 Lloyd George had the most impressive array of policies, but not even he could effectively stem the decline of the Liberals. Oswald Mosley in 1930 had an attractive economic strategy but could not overcome Labour loyalty to the party leadership. Even so, parties were not fixed or frozen and neither was the House of Commons. The 'pessimists' have pointed out the continuity in personnel in the Commons, as if the institution were becoming fossilised, but the 'optimists' have pointed to signs of change. At the end of the interwar period the Labour party was a much more diverse group than it had been at the beginning, and so were the Conservatives. In 1914 63 per cent of Tory MPs had been landowners; but by 1939 that figure had declined to 37 per cent. In 1914 22 per cent had careers in the armed forces or other official services; by 1939 this had been cut to 10 per cent. Over the same period, Tory MPs with careers in commerce and in banking rose from 12 per cent to 21 per cent. Parliament did not by any means mirror British society, but it was at least beginning to reflect the important socio-economic changes that were occurring.

It is often claimed that Britain sacrificed economic success for political stability, and there is much evidence to support this contention. However, it should be recognised that the new economic ideas might not have worked and that, in any case, a considerable amount of economic modernisation was achieved in Britain before the Second World War. But political success was not simply due to the party structure. It also owed much to the unity of the British nation and to the efforts of the politicians, who adapted themselves to the new situation. In particular they learned, with varying degrees of success, to use the radio and newsreels in order to inform and persuade the British public about their policies.

e) The Growth and Survival of Democracy

There is a vital element of success in the interwar years (so long, that is, as one accepts that democracy is a 'good thing') – the growth and survival of British democracy. The franchise was successfully extended to everyone over 21, so that women became part of the 'political nation'. We may deplore the fact that more women did not become MPs (their number peaked at 15 in 1931), but even so the democratic experiment worked in Britain. The country became a real democracy for the first time, and the machinery of British government survived in a period when democracy was collapsing in a large number of other countries. The British electorate did not become cynical and the overwhelming majority of voters turned out at every general election. Mosley's Fascist Union recruited a maximum of only 50,000 members, and about the same number joined the communist-inspired National Unemployed Workers' Movement. In other words, each of these bodies attracted little more than 0.1 per cent of a British population of almost 50 million. The official Communist party, despite a few well-publicised converts, achieved even less general support. The challenge from the extremes of left and right was an important aspect of the 1930s, making this decade an exciting one politically, but it should be remembered that the level of their support was statistically insignificant.

Britain entered the Second World War as a democratic nation and fought against totalitarian enemies for almost six years. At the end of the war in 1945, in the first general election for a decade, Winston Churchill insisted that Britain's political liberties were under threat. No one believed him. Everyone took British democracy for granted – that is a measure of how deep-rooted and successful it had become in the interwar years. But historians should not similarly take for granted this crucial success of the interwar years, the establishment and maintenance of democracy in Britain.

Yet how much credit should go to interwar politicians for the success of democracy in this period? This has so far been an insufficiently debated question. The 'critics' or 'pessimists' might well say that democracy flourished largely because of factors outside the politicians' control – the long-standing traditions of parliamentary government in Britain and the pattern which had grown up in the nineteenth century of extending the franchise to wider groups. Politicians after 1918 may also have been lucky, in that the undemocratic challenge, from extreme left and right, was relatively weak, especially because the depression from 1929 onwards did not reach a sufficient depth to produce a strong reaction against the political system. Yet the 'defenders', on the contrary, would insist that the survival of democracy was not inevitable and would therefore highlight the crucial and successful role played by the interwar politicians themselves. Labour politicians chose to abandon 'direct action' and to commit themselves to fostering evolutionary socialism through a moderate, reformist parliamentary party, while politicians like Baldwin managed to convince the voters that they could be trusted. They also managed to cope with the problems that beset the country well enough to prevent widespread disillusionment.

5 The Need for a Balanced Account

KEY ISSUE What overall verdict should we accept?

We must all make our own provisional judgements about the interwar years in Britain. Those who refuse to be partisan and adopt a middle position are often accused of 'sitting on the fence'. But this is often an unfair criticism. After all, one can take a very *decided* middle position (and sometimes a fence provides the best possible vantage point to see the surrounding areas). Decide how far you agree with the tentative conclusions contained in the following paragraphs.

The 1918–39 period is a highly controversial one and its significance in British history is very hard to assess. The 'pessimists' (employing criteria with which you should now be familiar) insist that the interwar years led nowhere except to the Second World War and that these were wasted years. Many have sensed a certain purposelessness about the interwar period, as though the politicians had no real goals for which to strive, other than their own continuation in power. There is much that is valid in this view. Yet the 'optimists' (with their different criteria) respond that, on the contrary, democracy was first instituted in this period and that it flourished, that Britain survived the great depression and successfully reoriented its economy and thereby minimised inevitable economic decline. The 20 years between the wars saw intense political debate in Britain which has been mirrored by historians of this period. Both sides have highlighted different aspects of these decades – both are right, but not exclusively right. The opposing views are complementary.

There was continuity and change between the wars. There was affluence and there was poverty, success and failure. It was 'the best of times' and 'the worst of times'. There was profound political stability and there was the crisis that led to the national coalition in 1931. There was a real commitment to democracy, but there was a growth of undemocratic parties on the left and the right. It was essentially a paradoxical period. Some opportunities were missed, but Britain did not resume in 1939 where it had left off at the end of the First World War. Far from it.

The events and developments of these years may well be viewed differently by historians in the future, as historical judgements rarely remain static. At present a favourable view of the interwar years is becoming more popular, redressing the balance following the exaggerated criticisms of the past (and perhaps reflecting the rightward trend of British politics during the 'Thatcher years'). But of one judgement we may be sure. Historians will always look upon the years 1918 to 1939 as ones worthy of study, and never to be dismissed as merely 'years in between'.

Working on Chapter 7

Far more important than compiling a detailed set of notes on this chapter is ensuring that you have an understanding of a) the range of views about the politics of the interwar period, and b) the criteria by which judgements are most frequently made. Why not construct a 'study-diagram' to sum up the two broad schools of thought, with their positive and negative assessments?

Throughout the chapter you have been challenged to formulate your own judgements – and now is the time to do so. What provisional conclusions have you reached on the sub-divisions of the interwar period made in the text and on the period as a whole?

To concentrate the mind, it is worth thinking about the following essay title:

1. Discuss the view that the interwar years in Britain were a time of mediocrity during which politicians 'marked time' instead of grappling with the fundamental problems that beset the country.

You should by now have realised the need a) to compose first paragraphs for essays, and b) to break down a large issue into smaller, more manageable ones. These involve skills which improve with practice. Remember that you do not have to have the same views as the author of this book and that your notes from this chapter should serve only as a guideline. The details needed for the essay should be taken from earlier chapters.

Further Reading

Two of the best general textbooks on the period covered by this volume are:

C.L. Mowat, *Britain between the Wars* (Methuen paperback, 1972)
A.J.P. Taylor, *English History, 1914–45* (Penguin, 1970).
Mowat's book is the more detailed and sound, and Taylor's the more controversial and provocative. Both, while daunting in size, are excellently written. A third should also be added:
Peter Clarke, *Hope and Glory: Britain 1900–1990* (Penguin, 1996).
The sections on the interwar period are not as detailed as those in Mowat's or Taylor's book, but Clarke shows the degree to which mainstream historical judgements have changed. He has also written an attractive and stimulating volume.
Robert Blake, *The Decline of Power, 1915–64* (Granada, 1985), is also eminently readable. His interpretations are generally far more sympathetic on the interwar politicians.
Keith Laybourn, *The Rise of Labour* (Edward Arnold, 1988), covers the inter-war period in chapters 4–6 and has a particularly strong coverage of historiographical debate. Also good on Labour between the war is **Andrew Thorpe**, *The History of the British Labour Party* (Macmillan, 1997). **Thorpe**'s *Britain in the 1930s* (Blackwell, 1992) is also highly recommended as an engaging and readable introduction to the period. For the Conservatives, an excellent introduction is **Stuart Ball**, *The Conservative Party and British Politics 1902–1951* (Longman, 1995).

Short biographies that students would find interesting include:
Kenneth O. Morgan, *Lloyd George* (Weidenfeld and Nicolson, 1974)
Kenneth Young, *Baldwin* (Weidenfeld and Nicolson, 1976)
Austen Morgan, *J. Ramsay MacDonald* (Manchester University Press paperback, 1987)
Duncan Watts, *Stanley Baldwin and the search for consensus* (Hodder & Stoughton, 1996)

Among the more 'heavyweight' publications, the following are important:
K.O. Morgan, *Consensus and Disunity: the Lloyd George Coalition, 1918–22* (Clarendon Press, 1979)
John Ramsden, *The Age of Balfour and Baldwin, 1902–40* (Longman, 1978)
Keith Middlemas and John Barnes, *Baldwin* (Weidenfeld and Nicolson, 1969)
Robert Skidelsky, *Politicians and the Slump: the Labour Government of 1929–31* (Penguin, 1970)
Maurice Cowling, *The Impact of Labour* (CUP, 1971)

Maurice Cowling, *The Impact of Hitler: British Politics and British Policy, 1933–1940* (CUP, 1975)
David Marquand, *Ramsay MacDonald* (Cape, 1977)
John Stevenson and Chris Cook, *The Slump* (Cape, 1977)
Robert Skidelsky, *Oswald Mosley* (Macmillan, 1981)
Richard Thurlow, *Fascism in Britain* (Blackwell, 1986)
Ben Pimlott, *Labour and the Left in the 1930s* (Allen and Unwin, 1986)
Philip Williamson, *Stanley Baldwin: Conservative Leadership and National Values* (Cambridge University Press, 1999)
G.R. Searle, *Country Before Party* (Longman, 1995)
Nick Smart, *The National Government, 1931–40* (Macmillan, 1999)

All of these books are, in different ways, outstanding scholarly contributions to our understanding of the inter-war period. They are particularly recommended for degree-level students, but others would also profit from dipping into them.

Sources on 'Domestic Politics, 1918–39'
Two books are particularly recommended:
Lawrence Butler and Harriet Jones (eds), *Britain in the Twentieth Century: A Documentary Reader, vol. 1, 1900–1939* (Heinemann, 1994) – an excellent and varied collection of sources, visual as well as written; and
Keith Laybourn (ed), *Modern Britain Since 1906: A Reader* (Tauris, 1999) – a large proportion of the book is on the interwar period, and it contains extracts from historians' interpretations as well as from primary sources.

Index